Northern Ireland

A Journey with Alf McCreary

Published in 2004 for
Lagan Books

By
Appletree Press Ltd
The Old Potato Station
14 Howard Street South
Belfast
BT7 1AP

Tel: + 44 28 9024 3074
Fax: + 44 28 9024 6756
Email: reception@appletree.ie
Web-site: www.appletree.ie

Text © Alf McCreary
Layout and Design © Appletree Press Ltd

Editors: Jean Brown and Jim Black
Designer: Joanne Diffin
Production: Paul McAvoy

A catalogue record for this book is available from the British Library.

ISBN: 0 86281 914 8
AP3127

9 8 7 6 5 4 3 2 1

Photographic Credits:
© Irish Stock Library (pp 23, 27, 29, 34-35, 46, 53, 59, 60, 64-65, 68, 80, 81, 82, 83, 85, 87, 92, 94, 107,
108, 109, 110, 113, 115, 118, 119, 120, 121, 122, 126, 130, 131, 132, 133, 134, 136, 137, 138, 141, 142,
146, 147, 148, 149, 155, 158, 159, 162, 163);
© Northern Ireland Tourist Board (pp 12, 15, 17, 18, 21, 25, 33, 36, 38, 40, 42-43, 44, 45, 47, 48, 49, 52,
54-55, 56, 57, 58, 63, 67, 70, 84, 90, 91, 95, 101, 102, 103, 104-105, 107, 111, 112, 116, 123, 124, 125,
127, 149, 154, 164);
© Belfast Visitor & Convention Bureau (pp 13, 17, 20, 23, 24, 32, 36);
© The National Trust. Photographs by Roger Kinkead (pp 72-73, 128, 129, 152, 153);
© The National Trust. Photographs by Christopher Hill (pp 78, 88, 98, 100, 101, 106);
© The National Trust (pp 150-151);
© The National Trust. Photograph by Mike Williams (p160-161);
© Féile an Phobail West Belfast (p 41); © Christopher Hill (p 96-97);
© Joan Shannon (pp 61, 62, 67, 74, 76, 77, 78, 79, 85); © Joanne Diffin (p 114)
© Esler Crawford Photography (pp 26, 28, 30-31, 37, 39, 50-51, 71, 75, 86, 89, 93);
© Derry Visitor & Convention Bureau (p 69); © Ulster Museum (p 22);
© Ulster Folk & Transport Museum (pp 156, 157); © John Murphy (pp19, 148);
© Appletree Press Ltd (p 14); © Ulster Hall (p 16);
© Royal Ulster Agricultural Society (p 24); © Tom Thompson (pp 29, 155);
© Naomi Corrigan (pp 117, 121, 122); © David Kirk (pp 135, 139, 143, 144-145)

Photograph of the case of the mummy, Tjesmutperet, reproduced with the kind permission of the
Trustees of the National Museums and Galleries of Northern Ireland.

Cover: The Beach near Portrush. © Esler Crawford Photography
Back cover: Devenish Island. © Northern Ireland Tourist Board
Scrabo Tower. © Irish Stock Library

Northern Ireland

A Journey with Alf McCreary

LAGAN BOOKS

Contents

Dedicated to

Molly Tess McCreary

Introduction

When I was asked to write this book, I was pleased to be given the opportunity to look again at the Province which so many of us think we know, but which continues to impress us—and sometimes surprise us—with its great sweep of sheer beauty. There are the mountains in their various moods, the surging oceans and seas which batter the coastlines, the rivers and lakes with their rich natural life, the nooks and crannies of interest just off the highways, and the buildings—ancient and modern—which tell how the people of many past and also present generations have left their imprint on this unique land. There is also the rich contribution to the life of Northern Ireland by its people from all backgrounds, including writers, musicians, painters, sculptors, inventors, and many more-and not least its many "characters."

This journey is a reflection on the best of Northern Ireland and its people, while bearing in mind some of the dark past in our complex and sometimes brutal history. Yet there is much to celebrate in Northern Ireland, and not least the resilience, resourcefulness and warm-heartedness of its people. It is a timely journey around a Province which has been in shadow for far too long, but which is emerging into a hopefully brighter and better age where each one can begin to appreciate more the culture and contribution of the other.

It is hoped that this book will be of interest to those who are discovering Northern Ireland for the first time, or returning to it after previous visits. This is not meant to be a definitive tourist guide as such, as much tourist literature is already available elsewhere, but rather a gentle reflection on a journey around a Province which has much to offer the visitor, and those who live here. One of the surprises of local life is that so few people know their native land really well, and this is an opportunity for all of to share in a journey which attempts to celebrate the best of a Province and its people.

I would like to thank all those who made this book possible. They include those whose quotations are gratefully acknowledged; Tom and Alan Thompson of Lagan Books, who commissioned the project; editor Jean Brown and designer Joanne Diffin of Appletree Press who handled the production; my wife Hilary for her support in every way; and finally the people of Northern Ireland past and present who have helped to make the best, and to preserve the best, of this beautiful place.

Alf McCreary
Belfast, 17 March 2004

Chapter 1

No Mean City

" I waited nervously for a Corporation bus...and stared hard at a pretty woman who returned my gaze coolly, and then gave me a wink as her bus drove off. For me the essence of Belfast remains as seductive as a wink from an alluring lady who moves on before you realise that she will never be yours."

Alf McCreary

Left: Belfast City Hall in Donegall Square.

Above: The Harland and Wolff cranes, "Samson" and "Goliath".

These comments about Belfast, made a number of years ago, summarised my views about this attractive, maddening, lively, sometimes troubled but always fascinating city. My views have not changed. Belfast, with its exquisite setting between the sea and dark blue hills can be one of the most beautiful places on earth, yet in a moment its face can cloud with a passing storm, but eventually the sun shines through. The real Belfast is like the elusive lady on the bus—attractive and alluring, but always just out of reach. Yet one never gives up trying to find her.

The distinguished Irish actor, wit and writer Micheal MacLiammoir, once noted that Belfast had "a peculiar charm of its own. Perhaps it is the charm of disguise, for that is one of the first things you notice about it; it wears a mask. ...but for the blue mountains at the end of the streets, the quality of the light, the sigh of the wind, certain faces and voices, certain hints of melancholy and of magic lightly touching you as day passes into night, you might easily believe yourself to be in Bradford or Manchester." Belfast is neither of these—it is uniquely and magnificently itself.

This is a city of many moods and many faces, but the discerning traveller will soon penetrate beyond these disguises to discover a richness and a warmth that belies its sometimes no-nonsense exterior. It was E.M. Forster, the well-known novelist and critic, who noted "Belfast stands no nonsense... one could scarcely find a city which stood nonsense less." There is no nonsense indeed, but nevertheless there is a sense of fun, a rich dark humour, and a genuine friendliness for those people, visitors and others, who are prepared to take the city as they find it. Belfast has few airs, but many graces.

The best way to discover Belfast is to start at the City Hall and the neatly-landscaped gardens at the heart of Donegall Square which encapsulate the atmosphere and history of the city.

The tall, domed and beautiful building was erected by the city fathers at the end of the 19th century in a mood of pride and self-congratulation. It was completed in 1906 at the height of Belfast's commercial and industrial prosperity, even though the architect Sir Brumwell Thomas had to chase the Corporation for his fee.

At the beginning of the 20th century Belfast was no mean city. It had the greatest shipyard, ropeworks, tobacco factory, linen spinning mill, dry dock and tea machinery works in the world. Outside the City Hall, built of white Portland stone, an imperious statue of Queen Victoria stares down Donegall Place to underline the city's 19th-century self-important awareness of its achievement as part of the British Empire.

This sense of Imperialism was further emphasised by the unveiling in 1906 of a handsome statue in the City Hall grounds of a former Marquis of Dufferin. During his career he was Governor of Canada, British Ambassador to Moscow, and Viceroy of India. Within an all too short a space of time, however, this Imperial and commercial grandeur slipped away.

Above: The *Titanic* Memorial which is situated to the east of the City Hall.
Right: A front view of the City Hall including the statue of Queen Victoria.

To the east of the City Hall there is an unprepossessing statue which commemorates the sinking of the mythically invincible *Titanic* in 1912, thus proving that the then state-of-the-art technology was no match for the powers of Nature, allied to human error. Across the City Hall gardens is yet another grim reminder of the immense courage yet fallibility of human beings. The elegant War Memorial to the dead of two World Wars, and of other conflicts since, commemorates the sacrifice of Belfast and its people in war—not least at the Battle of the Somme where huge losses were suffered by the 36th (Ulster) Division. The Ulstermen's ill-fated charge out of their trenches and across the battle-field is portrayed by a large and dramatic painting outside the Lord Mayor's Parlour.

The City Hall has long played a pivotal role in the life of the Province. It was here that the stern citizens of Belfast and their doughty country cousins signed the Ulster Covenant in their own blood during the Home Rule crisis in 1912.

It was here, too, that King George V opened the first Northern Ireland Parliament in 1921. His words are still poignant. He said, "I speak from a full heart when I pray that my coming to Ireland today may prove to be the first step towards an end to strife amongst her people, whatever their race or creed." Even a brief visit to the City Hall and its environs provides a rich heritage for anyone who wants a cameo view of Belfast and its history.

Just around the corner from the City Hall, in Bedford Street, is the Ulster Hall, another local institution that has been at the heart of the local community for many decades. Though its catering facilities are medieval, its acoustics remain superb, and it retains its own special atmosphere. It has staged countless events ranging from political and religious rallies, to boxing and wrestling contests, and music from across the spectrum.

It is here that the excellent Ulster Orchestra, regarded as one of the best in the British Isles, performs with world-class musicians including Belfast's acclaimed flautist James Galway and pianist Barry Douglas. This same stage has been home, too, to other local artists of international repute, including the legendary Van Morrison, the singer Brian Kennedy, and late and lamented Derek Bell of The Chieftains. The Ulster Hall also contains the outstanding Mulholland Organ, regarded as one of the finest in these islands.

Beside the Ulster Hall is the Group Theatre which has been the focus for so many talented Amateur Dramatics groups in Northern Ireland, often staging work by the late Sam Cree and other local writers. For many years this theatre was the home of James Young, one of the most talented and popular actors and entertainers of his generation. "Our Jimmy", as he was known, had a sharp ear for the Ulster language and dialect, an observant eye for local behaviour, and a comic genius to help a troubled and divided community to laugh at themselves, as well as each other. In his unique way he made an inestimable contribution to better community relations in Northern Ireland before the term was invented by the bureaucrats.

The historic re-opening of the nearby Grand Opera House in 1980 after bomb-damage signalled the renaissance of the city's cultural life, after the bleak, early years of the Northern Ireland conflict. Despite the

The Mulholland Organ was presented as a gift to the people of Belfast in 1861 by one of the ex-Mayors, Andrew Mulholland. It was fitted by William Hill and is one of the oldest and original examples of classical organ-building still being regularly used in performances today. It reputedly cost 3,000 guineas, a huge sum for those days.

Above: The Mulholland Organ in the Ulster Hall.

Above: The Opera House at night.

The majestic Grand Opera House in Great Victoria Street was designed by Frank Matcham (1854-1920). The ornately beautiful Opera House continues to attract a wide variety of visiting artists and companies of high quality following its re-opening in 1980 after bomb-damage during the Troubles.

Left: Ornate details from the interior of the Opera House.

grim violence of those years, the landmark Europa Hotel, just south of the Grand Opera House, survived the stern test of many bombs and the arrival of hordes of foreign visitors, including the world's journalists—and, in 1995, the US President Bill Clinton. Happily, the Europa has also acclimatised itself to more normal times when tourists and other visitors have a better opportunity to explore the attractions of the city.

These include the unique Crown Liquor Saloon, opposite the Europa Hotel, which the former Poet Laureate John Betjeman described as "a many-coloured cavern".

The "Crown" also serves good beer and Guinness, to accompany a lunch of Irish stew in one of the gorgeous little "snugs" in that colourful cavern. This elaborate example of a high-Victorian public house was featured in the 1946 classic movie thriller Odd Man Out which starred James Mason as an IRA gunman on the run in Belfast.

It was directed by Carol Reed in his prime, and was superbly filmed, with performances by the Irish actor Cyril Cusack and Belfast's playwright and actor Joseph Tomelty, both of whom would have known "The Crown" at first hand. According to popular tradition, the creator of "The Crown" was an ardent Irish nationalist, and his wife was a strong loyalist. It is said that she insisted on giving the pub its name, but he retaliated by depicting a crown in mosaic tiles at the entrance so that the patrons would walk over it. Since 1979 the Crown Liquor Saloon been owned by the National Trust, and as such it remains a treasure.

Another Belfast landmark, beyond the Crown Liquor Saloon, is the "Golden Mile". It stretches from the Grand Opera House and the Europa along Great Victoria Street, through Shaftesbury Square—with its distinctive iron sculptures high on the wall of a bank dubbed by the locals "Draft and Overdraft"—and on to Queen's University in the leafy suburbs of South Belfast. In and around this Golden Mile is a plethora of restaurants and pubs with a great variety of food and refreshments. This is a place to explore at night to sample the ambience of a lively city at play, though at weekends it can be frenetic.

The main Queen's University building is a magnificent redbrick structure, designed by one of Ireland's leading 19th-century architects, Sir Charles Lanyon. Opened in 1849, just in time for a brief visit from Queen Victoria herself, it was one of three "Queen's Colleges" established in Ireland in 1845—the others were situated in Cork and Galway.

Queen's obtained its University Charter in 1908, and today it is still one of the best in the British Isles, with a high national and international reputation for teaching and research.

Catering for some 25,000 full-time and part-time undergraduate and post-graduate students, it is also a university at the heart of the local community. A former Chancellor and Vice-Chancellor Lord Ashby once noted memorably that Queen's graduates touched the lives of every Ulster family, as a doctor or dentist or teacher or lawyer.

The list of Queen's Alumni since the mid-19th century is most impressive and it includes, from the recent past, outstanding men and women who have made their mark on the political, social, church,

Above: Exterior of the Crown Liquor Saloon.

Left: Queen's University designed by Sir Charles Lanyon.

Above: The Great Hall at Queen's University.

Above: Lord Kelvin statue at the entrance to Botanic Gardens.
Right: The Palm House at Botanic Gardens.

commercial, cultural and sporting life of Ireland, and much further afield. They include a President of Ireland, Mary McAleese, Professor Frank Pantridge, the pioneer of the world's first cardiac ambulance and Seamus Heaney, the poet and a Nobel Laureate in Literature. Others include David Trimble, a Nobel Peace Laureate and the inaugural First Minister of the Northern Ireland Assembly, Archbishop Robin Eames the Church of Ireland Primate and Archbishop of Armagh, Dawson Stelfox, the mountaineer who conquered Everest in 1993 by way of the treacherous North Route, and many more...

Culturally, the University has contributed greatly to the life of the Province. It founded the pioneering Queen's Film Theatre, and also established the Belfast Festival at Queen's which takes place each autumn and which has established itself as one of the premier arts festivals in these islands.

Just beyond Queen's are the Botanic Gardens, just one of the several attractive parks that provide green space and beauty, in and around this crowded city. The Gardens are a summer oasis for those seeking the sun (when it actually shines over Belfast), and they have been the venue for many events, ranging from band concerts to food-fests, and from pop concerts and to evenings of classical music among the greenery.

On the edge of Botanic Gardens the statue of Lord Kelvin, an outstanding 19th-century Belfast-born scientist, is a reminder of the innovative brilliance of a city and province that has produced such luminaries as John Boyd Dunlop, the inventor of the pneumatic tyre, Dr Thomas Andrews, a former Vice-President of the Queen's College whose work on chemistry was to lead eventually to inventions like the refrigerator, and Harry Ferguson, who invented the tractor.

The Ulster Museum has around 2,000 objects from ancient Egypt including the case of a mummy, a woman named Tjesmutperet. The exhibit was donated to the Belfast Natural History and Philosophical Society in 1845 by Sir James Emerson Tennant, who obtained the mummy in Thebes on his way home from his post of Civil Secretary to the Governor of Ceylon (now Sri Lanka). The mummy has been dated to c.650 BC and was found in the entrance to the Valley of the Kings.

Above: Details from the case of the mummy, Tjesmutperet.
Left: Case of the mummy Tjesmutperet, Thebes, c.650 BC.

Above: The Ulster Museum.

William Conor (1881 1968) is often called "the people's painter" of Belfast. Famous for his scenes of Belfast working-class life he captured the "Shawlies", mill girls and shipyard workers as they went about their lives. His former studio, now the Conor Café, is situated in Stranmillis Road, rather appropriately, opposite the Ulster Museum which displays some of his work.

Above: The Conor Café, formerly the site of William Conor's studio.

Just south of the Botanic Gardens is the Ulster Museum, with its unique collection of paintings by Ulster artists including William Conor, Andrew Nicholl, Paul Henry and Sir John Lavery. Opposite the building there is, appropriately, the Conor Café, which is the site of the artist's former studio.

The Ulster Museum (the Foundation Stone of which was laid in 1924 by the then Duke of York, later King George VI) has been known to generations of school-children because of its Egyptian Mummy—named Kabouti—in the Non-Irish Antiquities Gallery. The Museum also has an important Engineering Hall and Textile Gallery featuring industrial archaeology, with some of the artefacts representing Belfast in its golden years of engineering, and the Province's once-flourishing linen and textile trades.

The Museum also contains a fine collection of coins, as well as gold and silver jewellery and other memorabilia from the Spanish Armada vessel *Girona*, which sank in severe storms off the Giant's Causeway in 1588. The Museum also features many special exhibitions, including in recent years the paintings of Sir John Lavery and Frank McKelvey. This is a place where the visitor can learn much about the creativity and culture of Northern Ireland, and it has a good café for those who need a pit-stop on their journey of discovery.

From the upper-floors of the Museum there is also a good view of the ornate Palm House, with its impressive sweep of curved glass and iron-work, as well as the Tropical Ravine with its warm exotica in the heart of an often chilly city. Visitors to the Ulster Museum can also catch a glimpse of the historic Friar's Bush graveyard, which contains the remains of several distinguished Belfast citizens, including three newspaper proprietors and editors. Here, too, is the grave of the late Bernard Hughes, the city's first Roman Catholic Councillor and the proprietor of the bakery which produced the famous "Barney's Baps."

Several miles south of the University is the residential area of Balmoral and the King's Hall, which was built as part of an unemployment relief scheme during the Depression. Each year in May the Balmoral Showgrounds are the venue of a multi-faceted Royal Agricultural Show when most of Ulster's farming and associated industries are on display.

Not far from Balmoral the beauty of the Ulster countryside is a haven from the busy city, and the road leads to the Sir Thomas and Lady Dixon Park in Upper Malone. This vast green expanse is also a vivid array of colour each year when thousands of roses are on display for the prestigious City of Belfast International Rose Trials.

Near Dixon Park is Barnett's Demesne, a large park and the attractive Malone House formerly owned by William Barnett, a local grain merchant and breeder of successful racing stock. In 1929 his Trigo was the first Irish-owned horse to win The Derby.

The Barnett Demesne sweeps down to Shaw's Bridge and the River Lagan, where well-maintained paths for cyclists and walkers border both sides of the river. This is a particularly attractive haven of peace all the year round, with abundant bird-life and water activity amid the changing vistas of the seasons, in the south of the city.

Above: The Art Deco entrance to the King's Hall.

Above: Shaw's Bridge.

Right: The elegant interior of Malone House.

Above: The Sir Edward Carson statue.

Left: Stormont Demesne and Parliment Buildings.

Over in East Belfast, in the heart of the Stormont Demesne, is the seat of Northern Ireland government.

Due to the instability of local politics, Stormont has had more Assemblies and Executives than any other region of the British Isles in the last few decades. It remains, however, an imposing edifice set in acres of parkland which walkers can explore, though the building itself is not generally open to the public.

At the heart of the Stormont estate is the statue of a strident Sir Edward Carson, the Dublin-based lawyer who played a leading role in opposing Home Rule and thereby maintaining Ulster's political and constitutional link with Westminster.

The way back to the city centre leads through the heartland of east Belfast, with its striking and artistically distinctive wall-murals indicating the passionate loyalty to all things British in this part of the city. Here, too, are the dominant bright yellow cranes of Harland and Wolff dubbed "Samson" and "Goliath" which pay tribute to generations of workers and management at the shipyard.

It was some of these men who built and launched the *Titanic*, which like the tall yellow cranes on the shipyard site, still dominates the historical landscape nearly a century after its tragic and so unexpected demise. These cranes are among the tallest and most impressive in the world, and are arguably Belfast's best-known

landmarks. The dry dock is also one of the largest in the world.

Despite the continuing world-wide fascination with the *Titanic*, the city where it was built has been slow to give sufficient recognition to the historical and contemporary significance of a vessel which will live on in the collective memory for generations to come.

The shipyard was established at the Queen's Island in 1861 by the Yorkshireman Sir Edward Harland and his German partner Gustav Wilhelm Wolff. Sir Edward was the city's Lord Mayor in 1885 and he is commemorated by a statue outside the City Hall. The Harland and Wolff shipyard became one of the most famous in the world, and from the start it was innovatory in its design and production.

As well as the *Titanic*, Harland and Wolff launched a host of other historic vessels including *HMS Belfast*, which is now moored as a

Above: A colourful mural in East Belfast.
Left: Harland and Wolff cranes beside the Lagan Weir.
Next Page: The Belfast skyline.

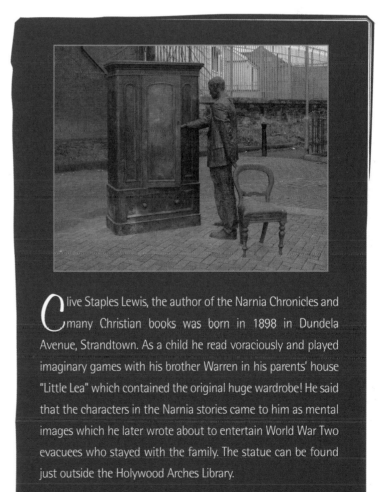

Clive Staples Lewis, the author of the Narnia Chronicles and many Christian books was born in 1898 in Dundela Avenue, Strandtown. As a child he read voraciously and played imaginary games with his brother Warren in his parents' house "Little Lea" which contained the original huge wardrobe! He said that the characters in the Narnia stories came to him as mental images which he later wrote about to entertain World War Two evacuees who stayed with the family. The statue can be found just outside the Holywood Arches Library.

Above: Statue in honour of C.S. Lewis, the creator of Narnia.

tourist attraction on the river Thames in London; the *Southern Cross*, which was the first ship to have a rear engine-room thus leaving more accommodation space for passengers; the cruise ship *Canberra*, which played an important role in the Falklands War as a troop carrier; the huge oil tanker *Myrina*, and in recent years a series of maritime structures including *Sea Quest* for the oil industry. Some experts believed that such a structure could not be launched, but Harland and Wolff managed to do so!

Not far away from the shipyard is the engineering complex of Short Brothers which is one of the oldest yet most technologically advanced aircraft companies in the world.

Shorts, as it is popularly known, produced the Sunderland Flying Boats as well as the world's first vertical take-off jet the SC-1, and the Shorts 360 commuter aircraft, the latter two are on display in the Ulster Transport Museum. The company is now owned by the Canadian company Bombardier. Nearby is the newly-refurbished Belfast City Airport with frequent commuter flights to the United Kingdom and other destinations.

Belfast and the sea are inseparable. Its story is that of the coastline and rivers which helped to shape the city. Its profile has been etched in the hard graft of workers and managers in commerce, textile manufacture, engineering and aircraft, as well as in shipbuilding. The city owes its name to its origin as "Beal Feirsde", the "mouth of the crossing." The River Farset, a tributary of the Lagan, takes its name from a sandbank or ford in the area.

The River Lagan itself, on its long journey from its source in the Mountains of Mourne, flows through the heart of the city and near the old Gasworks site which is now an attractive and rejuvenated business park. The Lagan also flows past the modern Hilton Hotel, and the view from the Lagan Lookout provides a broad vista of the harbour area and the new computer-controlled Lagan Weir. The river, which used to be smelly and dirty, has been rejuvenated and is now a centre for water-sports and boat-trips.

The Lagan glides past the new architecture of the Waterfront Hall, officially opened by Prince Charles at the end of the previous Millennium, and acknowledged to one of the best concert-halls in Europe. Just across the river, too, is the spacious Odyssey complex. This is the home of the ice-hockey team, the Belfast Giants, and it is an attractive modern complex for a multitude of major sporting, cultural and community events. There is a very good view of all these modern buildings and of the harbour itself, from the M3 motorway which sweeps majestically across the city at this point.

Above: The entrance to the Waterfront Hall.
Below: The Belfast Giants in action.

Right: The Odyssey Complex, home to the Belfast Giants.
Next Page: The Belfast Waterfront Hall at night.

Back across the Lagan, on the city side, is the elegant Custom House, also designed by Sir Charles Lanyon in the 19th century.

The magnificent sculpture of Neptune, Brittania and Mercury on the seaward side of the building looks across to the harbour. Not far away is the attractive Harbour Office, completed in 1895 with its grand stair-case and its paintings of local dignitaries and former cross-channel ferries which plied regularly to and from Britain, as some still do. Here, too, are some of the best-known pubs in Belfast, which are rich in hospitality and Irish traditional music. They include The Rotterdam, Pat's Bar and The Liverpool.

Belfast has so many other pubs of character and quality, that the visitor could literally become lost in their many delights. Among the best-known are Kelly's Cellars in Bank Street, which dates from the late 18th century, the early 19th-century Morning Star in Pottinger's Entry and McHugh's, near the docks, which has antecedents from the early 17th century but also an attractive air of modernity.

Near the heart of old Belfast is the re-furbished St. George's Market, and the Albert Memorial, known popularly as the "Albert Clock", which has also been restored to its former glory. Each year many of the New Year revellers who congregate here are in no condition to notice that this beautiful clock-tower is more than ever-so-slightly tilted, hence its nickname of "Belfast's Leaning Tower."

Across from the Albert Memorial is St. George's Church, built on the site of an early chapel of the first church in Belfast, and noted for its excellent music and for its high-church liturgy which is arguably the highest in the entire Church of Ireland. It is situated at the end of High Street, a part of Belfast which suffered enormous damage from the German air-raids on 1941 when more than 1,000 citizens of Belfast perished. The High Street area was re-built and is a thriving business centre.

In Royal Avenue there is the Castle Court Centre, a well-designed modern shopping complex. It was established on the former site of the historic Grand Central Hotel, which itself was built of local sandstone. This was also part of the area of the Old Smithfield, so beloved of bookworms and bargain hunters. The opening of the Castle Court shopping centre underlined the resilience of a city and its people in overcoming the ravages of the Troubles, and further refurbishment in the Cathedral Quarter nearby is envisaged.

Part of the heart-beat of any city is its newspapers, and at the end of Royal Avenue is the *Belfast Telegraph*, the province's leading daily

Above: The familar sign of the *Belfast Telegraph*, founded in 1870.

Left: The Albert Memorial more popularly known as the "Albert Clock".

Right: The Custom House and the Big Fish sculpture designed by John Kindness..

which was founded in 1870. Around the corner in Donegall Street is the office of the lively and respected morning daily *The Irish News*. The *News Letter*, thought to be the oldest daily in the English language, was once established further along, on Donegall Street, but some years ago it moved to a business estate in south Belfast.

Given the number of journalists working in and near the head offices of the two other dailies, it is no coincidence that some of the best-known pubs in Belfast are situated in this area. They include The Front Page in Donegall Street, the former site of McGlade's—a haunt of all journalists at the height of the Troubles,—while in Donegall Street near the heart of the old *News Letter* plant there is the John Hewitt, named after one of Ireland's most revered and well-known poets.

Just around the corner is a distinctive building which once housed another Belfast daily *The Northern Whig*, now sadly defunct. However, a good restaurant and popular night-spot of the same name exists there today, and is distinguished by its remarkable collection of three Communist Revolutionary Statues, which once adorned the top of the Communist Party Headquarters in Prague!

In today's world, as ever, God and Mammon live side by side, and back along Donegall Street is St. Anne's Cathedral, a 20th-century building noted for its spacious interiors, religious services, civic commemorations, and good church music.

It was here that Dean Samuel Crooks started the annual Christmas charity sit-out. Clothed in a large black cloak he braved all kinds of weather to collect huge sums for distribution to local and overseas charities, and also earned the title of Belfast's "Black Santa". Happily, this annual "sit-out" continues to take place every year.

Belfast has many attractive churches of all denominations, including the maritime Sinclair Seamen's Presbyterian Church in Corporation Square, St. Malachy's Roman Catholic Church in Alfred Street, with its historic turrets and vaulted ceiling; the Clonard Church and Monastery in West Belfast just off the Springfield Road, with its attractive interior;

St. Mark's, Dundela in East Belfast where the famous critic and Christian writer C.S. Lewis once worshipped; St. Peter's Pro-Cathedral in West Belfast and the beautiful First Church of Christ Scientist, in the University area, which was designed by the celebrated architect Clough Williams-Ellis, and many more. The city has also had a series of distinguished Jewish Rabbis since 1870, and Belfast-born Chaim Herzog, the son of a local Rabbi, served for two terms as President of Israel.

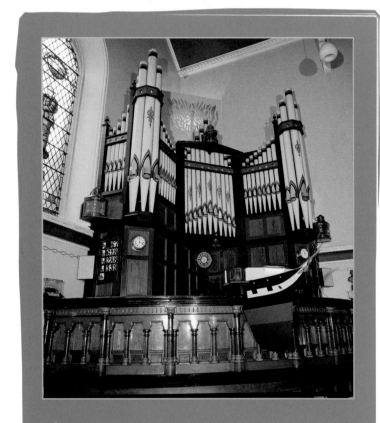

Sinclair Seamen's Church was designed by Charles Lanyon who was also the architect of the nearby Customs House. The classic exterior hides a maritime treasure trove inside which a pulpit is shaped with a ship's prow, the organ has port and starboard lights, the font is shaped like a ship's binnacle and even collection plates are shaped like lifeboats.

Above: Sinclair Seamen's Church celebrates Belfast's maritime history.

Right: The grand exterior of St Anne's Cathedral.

Moving West of the city centre along the Falls Road, there are more wall-murals which mirror the creativity of the Republican community in an area which has its own distinct vibrancy and way of life. This is where the ambitious and successful August Féile is held each year, and it opens with a colourful parade up the Falls Road almost to the Milltown Cemetery, which is noted for the historicity of its headstones and the well-kept graves in the Republican plot. This is well worth a visit.

Across on the Protestant Shankill Road, parts of which have been separated from the Falls by a so-called "Peace Line" during periods of unrest, there are yet more Loyalist wall murals proclaiming the political philosophy of an area that has had its own share of the Troubles. However, the spirit of the people remains strong, as is evidenced by the new hotel development of Farset International and the establishment and consolidation of the Farset Project, which helps to encourage and to develop job skills in an interface area of high unemployment.

To the North of the city is the grand sweep of the Cave Hill, an imposing outcrop which dominates the city, and directly overlooks Belfast Castle, a building in the Scottish Baronial style. Erected in 1870 and presented to the city by the Earl of Shaftesbury in 1934, it is now a well-known restaurant, and also a popular venue for wedding parties. The Castle grounds provide panoramic views of Belfast Lough and, further away, to the County Down countryside and the Mountains of Mourne.

The Castle woodlands also provide beautiful walks all the year round, and those who look for a sterner trek can eventually reach the summit of the Cave Hill, where near the top there are five man-made caves, dating from Neolithic times.

At the summit is McArt's Fort, named for an Iron Age chieftain and known locally as "Napoleon's Nose". It was here that in 1795 Wolfe Tone, Henry Joy McCracken and other United Irishmen pledged their loyalty to the cause of Irish independence from Britain. They swore "Never to desist in their efforts till they had subverted the authority of England over their country and asserted her independence." The repercussions of that pledge have not been settled even yet.

Despite the Troubles and the city's chequered past, there is hope for the future. Belfast retains its remarkable resilience, its sense of humour, and its capacity to surprise and to delight those who have an ear for dialect and street music, an eye for the unexpected, and the heart to greet this unique city and its people as they find them.

On the way out of Belfast, north of the Castle is the wooded hinterland of Bellevue, housing the impressive Belfast Zoo laid out on a steep mountainside but nevertheless readily accessible. The Belfast Zoo has established an international reputation for successes in breeding, particularly of endangered species. Its most noteworthy successes include the birth of a baby gorilla (only the second to be born in Ireland), and a baby Indian elephant in 1997.

From the slopes of Belfast Zoo there is the opportunity for a last, lingering look at Belfast—that attractive but elusive lady who always glides just out of reach—before moving north to Glengormley and on through County Antrim and one of the most beautiful and beckoning coastlines in the world.

Above: August Féile during the West Belfast Festival.

Left: Summer view of Belfast Castle.

Next Page: A final look over Belfast from the Cavehill.

Chapter 2

Travelling North

"But I'll spend my days an endless rover,
Soft is the grass I walk, my bed is free;
Ah, to be back in Carrickfergus
On that long road, down to the sea."

from the traditional song *Carrickfergus*

Left: The Giant's Causeway.

Above: Dunluce Castle.

The balladeer wished vainly to return to Carrickfergus but one person who did make the journey was Ulster poet Louis MacNeice, the son of a Church of Ireland rector in Carrickfergus. He often made the journey home from Belfast to this bustling town long ago and wrote the poem *Carrickfergus* about the experience. The journey is still pleasant and the drive along the Shore Road leads past the leafy residential suburb of Jordanstown and the University of Ulster, which was formed some years ago by the merging of the New University of Ulster and the former Ulster Polytechnic.

Carrickfergus is a small town crammed with history. Indeed, one of the official guidebooks makes no bones about its antiquity. It states "Carrick was a town of importance when Belfast was an unknown village on a Lagan mudbank. Its name goes back to the sixth century and was created by Fergus—an Ulsterman who was king of Dalriada in Scotland."

The silhouette of the town is dominated by the magnificently preserved twelfth-century Anglo-Norman Castle. This was built to guard the entrance to Belfast Lough, and the visitor with a keen eye can still spot the life-size models of soldiers on the battlements who look out for trouble, just in case!

Carrickfergus Castle has a stern history. It was built by John De Courcy, the Earl of Ulster between 1180 and 1204, and it was a much sought-after prize down the centuries by the warring factions of Normans, French, Scots and native Irish. In May 1315 Edward Bruce landed with a large army near Larne, and in the resultant fierce fighting the then Earl of Ulster—Richard De Burgo—was defeated at the Battle of Connor. His remnant army sought refuge in Carrickfergus Castle, but was forced to surrender after a year-long siege involving great hardship.

The Castle is much more mellow today as it looks over the bustling little harbour and marina, with its memorabilia of former days. It was here that King William of Orange landed in 1690 on a mission which led to the Battle of the Boyne and the eventual creation of a new political order in these islands.

William is commemorated by a black statue beside the Castle walls, and although he was by all accounts a good leader and a brave soldier, he was a diminutive figure—and this is reflected by his statue. Further along the quay there is a plaque to another monarch, Queen Elizabeth II, who landed in Carrickfergus in 1961. The Royal roots of Carrickfergus go deep.

Despite its formidable appearance, the Castle was captured by a marauding French fleet in the mid-eighteenth century, and in 1788 the American invader Paul Jones and his ship *Ranger* cheekily sailed up the Lough past Carrickfergus to capture *HMS Drake*—much to the consternation of the locals. However, the darker side of history is mostly left to the past, and the Castle stages medieval banquets as a tourist attraction, as well as the Lughnasa Fair each summer.

St. Nicholas' Church, in the town centre, also dates from the twelfth century. Despite the unwelcome attention from earlier invaders of the town, it has survived with style, and its crooked "skew" in the aisle is meant to symbolise Christ's head on the cross which was thought to have fallen to the right. The Church also has fine stained-glass windows.

Left: Statue of King William of Orange who landed at Carrickfergus in 1690.
Right: Carrickfergus Castle and harbour.

A particularly interesting feature of the town is the Gasworks Museum, which traces the origin and history of Carrick's former Victorian coal gasworks, the only one of its kind in Ireland.

Carrickfergus repays even a short visit. Its exceptional castle and picturesque harbour symbolise its motto "Gloria Prisca Novatur" (The Glory of Old Made New), and are reminders that the town is part of the very fabric of Ulster life.

Today the name of the town remains famous due to the beautiful and haunting folk-song called Carrickfergus, which has been performed and recorded by countless artistes around the world, and none better than the version by Ulster's Van Morrison.

Just north of Carrickfergus is Kilroot, once the residence in the mid-seventeenth century of the famous Dean Jonathan Swift who wrote *Gulliver's Travels* and—during his time at Kilroot—the *Tale of a Tub*. Nearby is the ancestral home of Andrew Jackson, the first American-born President of the USA, and one of some fifteen US Presidents of Ulster-Scots stock. His parents emigrated to the USA in 1765, and he was born in South Carolina two years later.

Near the site of their original homestead at Boneybefore is the Andrew Jackson Centre, which is a reconstruction of an eighteenth-century thatched cottage, with a small museum, which traces the strong links between Northern Ireland and the USA. The first battalion of the US Rangers was established in the Carrickfergus area in 1942, thus underlying the role played by US forces in the area prior to the Normandy landings in 1944.

Further north along the coast is Larne, which was a major military harbour for Allied troops during the war, and for many years its has been a major cross-channel port for freight and tourist traffic travelling to and from Northern Ireland. One of the greatest sea-tragedies of modern times occurred on 31 January 1953 when the *Princess Victoria* en route from Stranraer to Larne, foundered in a huge storm with the loss of 135 passengers. All the women and children perished.

Just north of Larne is Carnfunnock Country Park, and from here the Antrim Coast Road winds majestically all the way to Ballycastle. Beyond Drain's Bay and Ballgalley, with its Castle hotel, are the first signs of the Scottish coast which can be seen clearly on a good day.

The road travels through quaint Glenarm and on to Carnlough which has a picture-postcard harbour, and a wealth of history. The Londonderry Arms Hotel was built in 1848 as a coaching inn by the Marchioness of Londonderry, and eventually it was passed on to Sir Winston Churchill who made a visit during his short ownership when he was Chancellor of the Exchequer. The hotel retains its sense of history, as well as a reminder of the "sport of Kings" with a horse-shoe worn by Arkle when winning the Cheltenham Gold Cup in 1965.

Further north is Waterfoot, also called Glenariff, which provides good access to local waterfalls and woodlands, and these are a rambler's paradise. At Cushendall three of the nine Glens of Antrim converge—Glenaan, Glenballyemon, and Glencorp. The other six are Glenarm, Glencloy, Glenariff, Glendun, Glenshesk and Glentaisie.

Above: Carnlough Harbour.

Left: One of the waterfalls in Glenariff Forest Park.

Next Page: The famous Glens of Antrim.

In Cushendall there is a red Curfew Tower built in 1817 by Francis Turnly who was landlord of the village and who once worked for the East India Company. The tower was built to confine riotous prisoners or those who simply needed to sober up overnight. The abandoned ruins of Layde Old Church are nearby. The current building was established in 1306 AD and replaced an even earlier religious house. The ancient graveyard contains many old gravestones and a more recent beautiful Celtic cross erected in memory of Dr James McDonnell, co-founder of the hospital which would later become the Royal Victoria Hospital. To the north-west of Cushendall is Ossian's Grave, dating from Neolithic times, and there is also a Memorial Cairn to John Hewitt, the distinguished Glens poet who died in 1987. Each year there is a John Hewitt Summer School at St. MacNissi's College in Garron Tower, just a few miles south along the coast.

Above: The remains of Ossian's Grave, one of the heroes of Irish myth.

Right: Picturesque Cushendun, once a fashionable watering place.

Next Page: Torr Head overlooks Murlough Bay.

Still moving north, the traveller reaches Cushendun. This is another picturesque village with distinctive Cornish-style architecture by Clough Williams-Ellis, who designed the Italianate village of Port Meirion in North Wales. Incidentally Port Meirion became the location for the cult television series The Prisoner, which is still being broadcast regularly.

Another feature of Cushendun is the row of cottages which was built in 1925 in memory of Maud, the Cornish wife of Lord Cushendun who commissioned Clough Williams-Ellis. Not far from Cushendun is the distinctive Glendun Viaduct—designed by Sir Charles Lanyon, the architect of Queen's University and other outstanding buildings—and up on the moors is the "vanishing lake" of Loughareema.

The poet John Masefield once had a summer home in Cushendun. This later became a Catholic Retreat House. Here he may have mused more than once on his Epilogue, and remembered the poems in his *Salt Water Ballads* collection. Masefield loved the sea and even served a brief apprenticeship on a windjammer in the merchant navy, but he found the life hard and he later left his ship to live in the USA for a few years.

The final stretch of the Antrim Coast road brings magnificent views of Torr Head and Fair Head, and between the two lies Murlough Bay, which is one of the loveliest in Ireland. Here the visitor can sniff the bracing air during a brisk walk, or drive amid stunning scenery. A special feature of Murlough is the Stone Cross Memorial to Sir Roger Casement, the former colonial civil servant who was hanged for treason in 1916 after attempting to further Irish independence by enlisting the help of Germany against the British.

On the outskirts of Ballycastle are the ruins of Bonamargy Friary, founded by the Franciscans around 1500 AD, and these contain the remains of a local chieftain Sorley Boy McDonnell and his early descendants, the Earls of Antrim. Here, too, is the grave of a seventeenth-century recluse Julia MacQuillan, known as the "Black Nun." According to folklore she was murdered by a fellow priest. She was believed to have possessed the powers of witchcraft and reputedly forecast that human beings in machines would one day "travel through the sky."

The "Black Nun" was buried inside the entrance to the church, and this has various interpretations, like most things in Ireland! Some say that this was because she wanted worshippers to walk over her grave on their way in and out of the church, in order to remind them of her humility. Others believe that the grave was placed prominently at the entrance to the church to emphasise the fear in which she was held during her lifetime.

Not far from the Friary, on a beautiful hilltop overlooking Rathlin, is the Christian and inter-denominational Corrymeela Community Centre which, from the mid-Sixties, has been a focus for greater understanding among people of all backgrounds. During the Troubles and beyond it has lived up to its motto "It is better to light a candle than to curse the darkness."

The town has its share of good pubs, including McDonnells—dating from 1766—and the Antrim Arms, where Marconi lodged in 1898 when he carried out his first successful experiments on radio transmission across the six miles between Ballycastle and Rathlin Island. Photographs and other memorabilia adorn the lounge bar of the Antrim Arms.

In 1898 Lloyds of London commissioned Marconi to set up an experimental radio relay to report the movements of shipping between Rathlin and the mainland, because the old "Flag System" involving Torr Head was becoming outdated. Marconi's assistants George Kemp and Edward Granville were sent to Rathlin to prepare the experiments, but Granville fell of a cliff and died. Marconi arrived later and although the experiments were successful, the potential of radio transmission was not pursued commercially for some time. Marconi's important achievements are commemorated today by a handsome stone monument near the modernised harbour.

Rathlin Island, to the east of Ballycastle and only about 12 miles from the Mull of Kintyre, is a world apart. Once it was difficult to reach due to the treacherous tides which sweep between it and the mainland, but a modern ferry now makes the regular 40 minute journey with ease, though not without some turbulence.

The island has many attractions, particularly for the walker and for those who like bird-watching. One of the best sites for bird-watching is Bull Point where in mid-summer there are many thousands of

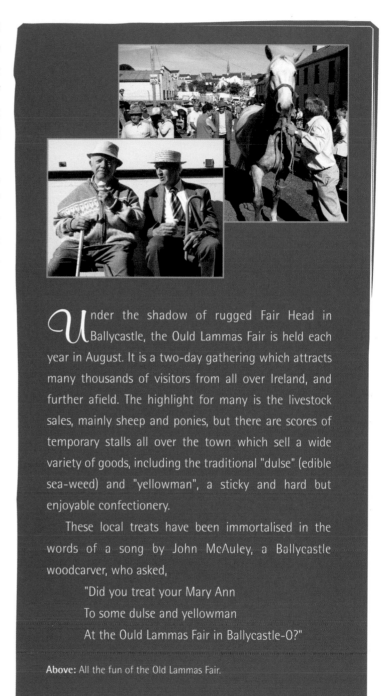

Under the shadow of rugged Fair Head in Ballycastle, the Ould Lammas Fair is held each year in August. It is a two-day gathering which attracts many thousands of visitors from all over Ireland, and further afield. The highlight for many is the livestock sales, mainly sheep and ponies, but there are scores of temporary stalls all over the town which sell a wide variety of goods, including the traditional "dulse" (edible sea-weed) and "yellowman", a sticky and hard but enjoyable confectionery.

These local treats have been immortalised in the words of a song by John McAuley, a Ballycastle woodcarver, who asked,

> "Did you treat your Mary Ann
> To some dulse and yellowman
> At the Ould Lammas Fair in Ballycastle-O?"

Above: All the fun of the Old Lammas Fair.

seabirds, including kittiwakes, razorbills, puffins and guillemots. After a long day's walk around mostly deserted roads, and often in bracing winds, the visitor can sample a good pint in the local hostelry, and even find suitable accommodation on the island for the night.

Left: Rathlin Island shoreline from the air.

Rathlin is rich in history and folklore. Perhaps its most famous story is that of Bruce's Cave where Robert the Bruce sought refuge after his defeat by the English. According to legend the despondent Bruce watched a spider try repeatedly to reach the roof of the cave by climbing its thread. At last it succeeded, and Bruce was inspired to "try, try, again." Thus motivated, he returned to Scotland, and defeated his enemies.

Rathlin has been the home of many different people—from farmers and fishermen to monks and smugglers. Its offshore waters hold the secrets of many naval wrecks, such as the *Drake* and *Lough Garry*, and its churches and graveyards have their own historic tales. In St. Thomas' Church of Ireland, near the shoreline, there are memorials to the Gage family who bought the island for only £1,750 in 1746, and also a faded black and gold tablet commemorating the valet of a German Prince on the island who had married a member of the Gage family. The lovely little Roman Catholic Chapel, tucked into the side of a hill, dates from 1865.

Back on the mainland, after the return ferry crossing, the visitor travelling north will enjoy a long, last look at the rugged beauties of Rathlin, and its memories, before passing the few remnants of Kinbane Castle and eventually stopping at the famous Carrick-a-Rede Bridge.

This is an intimidating structure made of planks and wires and strung across a usually churning sea to give salmon fishermen access to a small rocky island off the coast. People are warned of the risks in crossing but many are brave, or foolhardy, enough to make the journey—often accompanied by screams of fright during the crossing, and whoops of joy when it is completed. It all sounds rather frightening, but in reality it can be good fun, especially with like-minded adventurers, but more than a little caution is required when making the crossing each way.

Beyond Carrick-a-Rede, the road leads to the village of Ballintoy where an eighteenth-century landlord was called Downing Fullerton. He was a member of the family whose name is perpetuated in Downing

Above: The scant remains of Dunseverick Castle.

Right: Preparing to cross Carrick-a-Rede Bridge.

College, Cambridge, and Downing Street, London. Travelling on the winding road down to the picturesque Ballintoy Harbour, the visitor passes a small and beautiful white parish church, and further along is a remarkable house designed by the eccentric genius Newton Penprase. He was so much his own man that the spelt his surname with an "s", and not with a "z" like the rest of the family. Like the house he designed, he was unique.

Back on the main road, the traveller will pass the sparse remains of Dunseverick Castle, rich in legend and folklore. Dunseverick was the capital of the ancient kingdom of Dalriada, but sadly little remains, apart from the Castle itself. Beyond Dunseverick there is a good parking area at the edge of the cliff-top above the gorgeous outline of White Park Bay, this is in the care of the National Trust. Archaeological remains found in this area date back to 2,500 BC.

It is worth pausing here to enjoy the scenery, before talking the long walk down to the beach. Further on is the tiny settlement of Port Bradden which nestles at the bottom of a long, winding road which, nevertheless, gives good access by car. Its main feature, apart from a cluster of houses with panoramic sea views, is a tiny Anglican church which is the smallest in the Church of Ireland.

Not far from Carrick-a-Rede the visitor reaches the Giant's Causeway, which has been rightly described as "one of the eight wonders of the world."

This is a striking array of basalt columns and outcrops which were formed some 60 million years ago by the cooling of lava, though the locals of previous generations had a much simpler theory. They believed that the Causeway was built by the Irish Giant Finn MacCool who wanted to create a path across the sea to do battle with his Scottish counterpart! One of the particular attractions is Port Cuan (or Coon) which is a huge cave accessed by boat. Once upon a time the tourist guides would blow bugles so visitors could experience the dramatic echo inside the cave's Gothic proportions.

Despite the somewhat choleric view of Dr Samuel Johnson that the Giant's Causeway was worth seeing "but not worth going to see", it remains a major tourist attraction, and is a UNESCO World Heritage site. There is much geological history here, as well as outstanding sea views and challenging cliff-path walks which are rewarding but worthy of caution. The area is also in the care of the National Trust, which also owns the period Causeway Hotel nearby. It is well known for serving some of the heartiest food and drink in all of Ireland, including a "mixed grill" of gargantuan proportions which almost requires two plates per person!

Bushmills was also the focus of a hitherto little known story whereby a former revolutionary new navigational code developed by the German Luftwaffe and named "Consol" was captured by the British during the Second World War. It was later adapted as a key navigational aid for European aircraft in peace-time. The Consol system

The world-famous Old Bushmills Distillery dates from 1608, when Sir Thomas Phillips was granted a licence by King James I to make "aquavitae in the County of Colrane and the Route, Co. Antrim." Also known as "usquebagh" or "the water of life", whiskey creates its own history and folklore. Old Bushmills is now the world's oldest whiskey distillery still currently in production. The distillery is open to visitors and a guided tour—including a tot of the modern "water of life"—is recommended.

Above: Barrels at the world's oldest whiskey distillery.

was installed in a small building three miles outside Bushmills. It was opened in 1946 with the appropriate call signal "MWN-Mike-Whiskey-November", and for many years its 310 feet aerial masts were a feature on the Causeway Coast landscape until it was overtaken by new technology and closed down on 30 September 1976.

The system was switched off some 90 minutes before the official time of midnight—so that the "farewell party" would reach the bar at the Bay View Hotel in Portballintrae before closing time. The Bay View, a hostelry of character still entertains the weary or thirsty although the coastal village of Portballintrae has now been transformed by modern developments.

Left: The striking basalt columns of the Giant's Causeway.

West of Bushmills is Dunluce Castle, strikingly perched on an outcrop overlooking the North Atlantic. It was certainly too close to the beach for comfort in 1639, when part of the kitchens with all the pots and unfortunate servants were plunged into the sea during a severe storm. In recent years there were suggestions that a "Son et Lumiere" might re-tell the Castle's rich history, but thus far it has remained in relative darkness, apart from those evenings when a magnificent sunset etches the beauty of the Donegal coastline and throws long shadows across Dunluce and its history.

Near the Castle is the memory of more dark history, and in a small graveyard lie the remains of Spanish seamen who were washed ashore when the Armada vessel the Girona foundered off the Causeway Coast in 1558. There were only eleven survivors. The place where the bodies were washed ashore is still called Port na Spaniagh.

Another important feature of this part of the coast is the steam locomotive railway from the Causeway to Bushmills, which opened recently and is a popular tourist attraction as it weaves its way past pretty Runkerry beach and through the nine-hole but tricky Bushfoot Golf Course. This runs along the site of the older and famous Giant's Causeway Electric Tramway, established in 1883 as the world's first commercial hydro-electrical tramway. It proved successful for many years, but had to close in 1949 because it was losing money. The original Bushmills Station has survived although it is now a petrol station.

The town of Portrush is popular with day-trippers, and with those who wish to stay longer to appreciate the excellent beaches including the White Rocks strand, the superb golfing facilities, the good food and also the more traditional seaside treats. These including the well-known Barry's Amusements park which has thrilled successive

Above: The Giant's Causeway to Bushmills steam locomotive.

Right: Dunluce Castle perches on its dramatic clifftop home.

Next Page: A beach near Portrush.

Portrush has been the site of human habitation for over 1,500 years but its harbour really expanded in the early 19th century with the advent of the Industrial Revolution. Cargoes of timber arrived from America and local produce such as grain and potatoes were shipped to ports all over the Britain. Fish was also landed and then re-shipped to Belfast. The railway arrived in 1855 and with it, tourists eager to visit the Giant's Causeway and the north coast. The visitors still come to Portrush and its harbour and one of their favourite places since 1986 is Waterworld, the indoor water playground.

Above: Portrush Harbour shelters some tiny boats from the Atlantic.

generations of children—and their parents—during their own childhood. Each year there is another helter-skelter of nautical fun when hardy adventurers join the Raft Race across the harbour!

Portrush, to some extent, has a split personality. In the past it has been a classic resort, despite the Ulster weather which dampened many a family holiday. It still retains that "bucket and spade" atmosphere when the sun shines, but Portrush like other resorts in the British Isles has had to adapt to changing times when people can afford holidays with guaranteed sun elsewhere.

Portrush has started to move upmarket, with many new apartments being built, and also excellent dining in places like the Harbour Bar. It is also known internationally for its championship golf course which is one of the best in the world. The Royal Portrush Club hosted The Open Championship, which was won by Max Faulkner in 1961, and more recently it has been the venue for the prestigious Seniors Golf Championship, which features international professionals of an age rather higher than their handicaps!

Moving west, the road runs parallel to the coast, with commanding views of distant Donegal, and leaves the county of Antrim as it moves into County Londonderry or—as some call it—Derry, with its own scenic delights. Northern Ireland is a Province with many attractive faces, and in Londonderry—like Antrim—there is also much to celebrate.

INLAND ANTRIM

There are many attractions along the inland route in County Antrim. The town of Antrim itself has a tenth-century Round Tower in Steeple Park, and a delightful public park which was formerly the Massereene Demesne, and belonged to the local gentry. The excellent 18-hole Massereene Golf Course affords magnificent views across Lough Neagh, the largest inland lake in the British Isles, as well as those of Antrim Castle and the Sperrins in the far distance.

A special feature of Antrim is Pogue's Entry, the birthplace of Alexander Irvine who wrote the classic book *My Lady of the Chimney Corner*. Irvine and his parents are buried nearby in the All Saints' Parish Church, which has Renaissance stained glass and dates from 1596.

Further north is the prosperous town of Ballymena, the economic hub of mid-Ulster. This is associated with a wide variety of famous people and institutions, include the actor Liam Neeson, and successive Army regiments, including the current Royal Irish Regiment. Another famous name associated with Ballymena is Willie-John McBride, the former Ireland and British Lions rugby player.

Ballymena is also associated with Timothy Eaton who learned the drapery business in nearby Portglenone, and emigrated to Canada in the nineteenth century, where he established the well-known chain of department stores. It was said that for many years, Ulster people who emigrated to Canada were given a "start" with a job at Eaton's.

Modern Ballymena retains much of the character of an old-style country market town, but it has two of the best modern shopping centres in Northern Ireland—Fairhill and The Tower Centre.

At Gracehill, just west of Ballymena, there is a beautiful Moravian Church, dating from the eighteenth century. Each Christmas Eve the congregation holds a special "Christingle Service", during which small candles placed in oranges decorated with tiny sweets, are lit amid the afternoon gloom to herald the birth of Christ. Outside the church there is a well-laid out cemetery, where—according to Moravian custom—men are buried along one side, and women along the other. The silence, naturally, remains deafening.

In Ballymoney a museum is dedicated to Joey Dunlop, the famous motorcyclist who tragically died in 2000 during a race in Estonia. In an outstanding career, he won five Formula One World Championships, 26 Isle of Man TT Races, 10 Superbike victories at the Coca-Cola International North-West 200, and five World Titles for Honda. There is also a memorial garden in the centre of Ballymoney which features a full size bronze statue by the sculptress Amanda Barton of Joey astride the Honda motorbike on which he won the 2000 Isle of Man TT.

Ballymena is also the site of the ECOS centre which features educational displays on environmental issues. These are particularly suited to those with unquenchable scientific curiosity, and after a visit, those who have had enough food for thought can also relax along a number of walks around the 150-acre park.

Above: The ECOS centre on the outskirts of Ballymena.

Above: The Joey Dunlop Memorial Garden in Ballymoney.

Right: The tenth-century Round Tower in the Steeple Park.

Chapter 3

North Coast to Maiden City

"Oh Danny Boy, the pipes, the pipes are calling
From glen to glen and down the mountain side
The summer's gone and all the roses falling
'tis you, 'tis you must go and I must abide."

from the traditional song *Danny Boy*

Left: Mussenden Temple on its cliff-top home.

Above: "Hands Across the Divide" statue in Derry.

The haunting tune of *Danny Boy* was first heard near Limavady in County Londonderry and another evocative song also came from this county. *Red Sails in the Sunset* by Jimmy Kennedy describes a long mellow sunset across the Atlantic Ocean at Portstewart as the sun sinks over the hills of Donegal.

In such a setting, Portstewart is one of the most beautiful places on earth, and every time *Red Sails in the Sunset* is played—which is still quite often—it creates a picture of that mellow scene on the North Coast. He wrote the lyric of the 1935 song while looking out to sea from his parent's home in Strand Road, Portstewart.

Jimmy Kennedy was a prolific songwriter, with many international hits to his credit, albeit in another age when popular music was more tuneful and there were lyrics of sentimentality and beauty. His best-known songs include *South of the Border*, *Harbour Lights*, and many others, and today these are performed with panache by a local and mature male group called The Brassnecks. It is appropriate that Jimmy Kennedy is thus honoured in the area that inspired some of his best-known songs, and in Portstewart there is a 12-foot bronze sculpture of a boat in his memory.

Portstewart is altogether more sedate than her more brassy sister Portrush, and it is a favourite place for retirement.

However, it is much more than a huge retirement complex, and Portstewart has many attractions in its own right, including a well-kept promenade with some stylish shops, and Morelli's Cafe and Restaurant.

This Ulster institution was established by an Italian immigrant between the two World Wars, and the family business has prospered ever since, despite the challenges of each decade. One of the most-popular pastimes in Portstewart is to buy a coffee or ice-cream in Morelli's and to watch the world meander along the promenade outside.

This is a favourite resort for those who drive up in their cars, park them along the promenade and gaze out to sea, without putting a foot on the ground. More often than not the Sunday papers seem a bigger attraction to such people than the fresh Atlantic air, and the glorious scenery across the Foyle estuary to Donegal.

Above: Portstewart Promenade, a favourite Sunday location for many.

However, born ramblers have a wide choice of walks in this area. One of the best is along the cliff-path, and past the walls of O'Hara's Castle, an early nineteenth-century folly that was later converted into the now familiar Dominican Convent and school. The path leads past a herring-pond where locals still dive into the Atlantic in all weathers, and on to the magnificent Portstewart Strand.

Now in the care of the National Trust, this is one of the best beaches in Ireland, with sandhills on the left running down to the River Bann, and unspoiled views of Donegal. This strand affords a challenging walk to the Bar-mouth where the River Bann meets the sea. The beach is also open to motorists, but care should be taken when parking. There are many sad tales of drivers who parked too close to an incoming tide, with unfortunate consequences.

Near the beach is the testing 18-hole Portstewart Golf Course, while back beyond the promenade is another smaller, but neverthless tricky, 18-hole Old Course, where the first and tees and greens are situated virtually on the rocky coastline. Many a potentially good score has also been ruined on the way back to the club-house.

The middle part of the course lies across the main road, and near here is the start of the famous North West 200 motor-cycle race which is one of the world's fastest road races, and attracts top-class riders. Each year in May around 100,000 fans converge on Portstewart for the practice evenings and for the race itself, and it is one of the outstanding events in the annual sporting calendar in Ulster where motor-bikes have a huge following all the year round.

Despite its sedate reputation, Portstewart has much to offer the visitor, and its tidy harbour is one of the most picturesque in the land. On the way out of the town, towards Coleraine, the road leads past the Flowerfield Arts Centre and on past the campus of the University of Ulster, with its Riverside Theatre. Here, too, is the Guy L. Wilson Memorial Garden, which is dedicated to the memory of an outstanding Ulster daffodil breeder. Not surprisingly, the garden is ablaze with daffodils each Spring.

Coleraine has been described as "This most English of towns in Ulster", which is hardly surprising as its modern foundation dates from the seventeenth century as part of the Plantation of Ulster by, among others, the Companies of the City of London. In St. Patrick's Parish Church part of the transept and nave survive from the first settlement of 1613.

The attractive Town Hall dominates a square that has seen better days, though Coleraine remains a lively shopping centre. William Makepeace Thackeray in his famous *Irish Sketchbook* on 1842 noted that "Among the beauties of Coleraine may be mentioned the price of beef, which a gentleman told me may be had for fourpence a pound; and I saw him purchase an excellent codfish for a shilling." Clearly, Coleraine was always a good shopping centre.

The town has a notable antiquity that stretches far back beyond the seventeenth century. Coleraine is associated with a visit from St. Patrick himself in the fifth century. In Bishop Tirechan's "Life of St. Patrick" in the *Book of Armagh*, he states that Patrick "proceeded across the River Bann, and he blessed the place in which is the little cell of Cuile Raitin in Eilniu in which there was a Bishop, and he made many other cells in Eilniu and he built many churches which the Coindire (the bishops of Connor) possess." According to the author James Stuart who wrote the *Historical Memoirs of the City of Armagh*, published in 1819, Patrick also visited "Dunboo" in "the barony of Coleraine and the county of Derry."

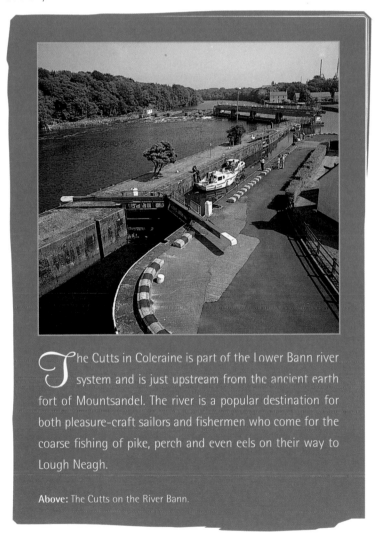

The Cutts in Coleraine is part of the lower Bann river system and is just upstream from the ancient earth fort of Mountsandel. The river is a popular destination for both pleasure-craft sailors and fishermen who come for the coarse fishing of pike, perch and even eels on their way to Lough Neagh.

Above: The Cutts on the River Bann.

Next Page: Portstewart Strand and the distant view of Mussenden.

Above: Ruins of Bishop's Palace.

The history of Coleraine goes back even further than St. Patrick, and at Mountsandel, above the River Bann, there is a 200-foot high mound that archaeologists claim to be the earliest habitation in Ireland, and which dates back some 9,000 years. Today there is a well-kept pathway at Mountsandel which provides excellent access to the historic site and also a delightful walk beside the river.

In this broad area of the Bann were found the ninth-century Dalriada Brooch and the second-century Bann Disc which is the emblem of the Ulster Museum and is kept there in its antiquities collection. On the inland route to Limavady is the "Murderhole Road" and the Giant's Sconce, with commanding regional views, as well as Second Dunboe, a charming little Presbyterian church, with a graveyard quiet enough to allow any writer

and his family to rest in peace.

The coast road out of Coleraine leads towards Articlave and on to Castlerock, an attractive seaside village with nowadays an air of affluence, a good golf course, and an even better beach. On the road just before the junction for Castlerock is Hezlett House, a thatched building dating from 1690—a date which, of course, has other associations in Ireland.

Beyond Castlerock on the road to Downhill is the entrance to the Bishop's Glen and Mussenden Temple. There are beautiful walks along the Glen and past the old Bishop's Palace, now in ruins, and on to Mussenden Temple, which is perched on an outcrop overlooking a long strand of beach.

This is one of the best-known structures in Northern Ireland, and was built in the late eighteenth century by Frederick Augustus Hervey, the 4th Earl of Bristol who was also the Church of Ireland Bishop of Derry. Known also as "the Temple of the Winds" because of its weather-beaten location, it was inspired by the temples of Vesta at Tivoli in Rome, and was named in honour of the Bishop's young cousin, the beautiful Mrs Mussenden—although she died before it was completed.

He was very much his own man, and in his day he was a champion of Catholic rights, and he made available the basement of the Mussenden Temple for Roman Catholic worship. He was also delightfully eccentric, and he once staged a horse-race on Magilligan Strand between Presbyterian and Anglican clergy.

Above: The Palace was built by the Bishop of Derry.
Right: Bird's eye view of Mussenden and Bishop's Palace.

There are magnificent sea views from Mussenden Temple, which is now in the care of the National Trust, and there is also a good path back to Castlerock. For the visitor moving further along the coast, the road winds down a steep hill to the hamlet of Downhill, and immediately left there is a steep climb on a minor road which leads to the Eagle's Nest. This affords one of the best views along the entire North Coast.

On the way to Magilligan, and past the Prison, the traveller will reach a new ferry that operates regularly across the Foyle estuary to Greencastle in Donegal. This cuts drastically the land journey to this area via Londonderry city, and is a boon to those who wish to make a quick visit to this hospitable part of Donegal—though all of Donegal is as delightful as it is hospitable. Day-trippers can enjoy a delightful excursion to Greencastle, via the ferry, a walk to nearby Moville for a snack, and back again by ferry.

Above: Ferry taking visitors across the Foyle to Co. Donegal.

Left: Magilligan Point—popular with visitors on foot or by boat.

Magilligan Strand, also known as Benone Strand, is one of Ireland's most magnificent beaches and has been granted the European Community's Blue Flag status for its cleanliness. At the western end of the beach is Magilligan Point, with a Martello Tower built during the Napoleonic wars to protect the narrow entrance to Lough Foyle.

This was the latest military technology available, and seemed formidable enough at the time. The technology, however, moved on, and some 130 years later the Tower was used to house the latest, and then secret, radar defence system for the Foyle Estuary during the Second World War. The Tower thus has the distinction of being a bastion of defence against potential European invaders down the ages, from Napoleon to Adolf Hitler, for some 200 years.

This broad region of the North Coast was part of the strategic defence system of the United Kingdom during the Second World War.

A number of military airfields were established in the area, including one at Eglinton, which is now the site for Derry City Airport; another was based at Maydown, which is now a major industrial estate; and a third was based at Limavady, which remains in private ownership.

The airfield at Ballykelly provided vital air support for the Allied naval base at Londonderry which itself was of paramount importance. This was the base from which the war was waged to protect the North Atlantic shipping convoys against German U-boat and other naval attacks, and which carried supplies for the survival of the United Kingdom, and helped to prepare the eventual Allied invasion of Europe. Derry was selected for the surrender of the German U-boats fleet at Lisahally, and this was a significant and symbolic milestone in the city's history. A War Memorial to those who died in the two World Wars is located in the Diamond area. During the Second World War, some 20,000 US military personnel were stationed in Londonderry and even long after the war, there was a distinct American dimension to the city.

Moving on from the Martello Tower, which led to the above military diversion, the tourist trail at Magilligan leads to nearby Bellarena, where the locally-based Ulster Gliding Club has access to some of the most soaringly-beautiful landscape views in Europe. Incidentally it was also at Magilligan Strand where the Ulster inventor Harry Ferguson tested his pioneering monoplane aircraft. A number of successful flights at Magilligan gave him the experience to accept a £100 challenge at an Aerial Display in Newcastle, Co. Down, "for the first person in Ireland to make a three-mile flight." He was the first person in Ireland to build and fly an aeroplane, in 1910. A replica is on display at the Ulster Folk and Transport Museum in Cultra.

The drive towards Limavady passes through attractive scenery, and the town itself has perhaps one of the best claims to fame in all of Ireland. It was the home of Jane Ross who lived at 51 Main Street, and in 1851 she had the presence of mind to jot down a tune from an itinerant fiddler. This became the hauntingly beautiful Londonderry Air, also known as Danny Boy and it is still probably the best-known and best-loved melody in the entire Irish repertoire. Incidentally one of the best versions recorded is that of the Irish singer Tommy Fleming.

Jane Ross and her three younger sisters are buried in the local eighteenth-century Parish Church, and there is also a plaque in memory of the early twentieth-century Prime Minister of New Zealand William Massey. South of Limavady is the Roe Valley Country Park, with an impressive collection of restored country buildings. The former Roe Park House, an early Georgian mansion built by a Speaker of the Irish Parliament William Conolly, is now a luxury hotel. The Park is popular with tourists, and has a good reputation for game fishing.

Above: Power House Museum in Roe Valley Country Park.

Right: Roe Valley Country Park.

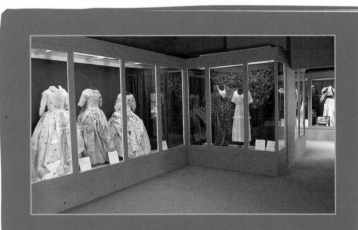

Springhill, near Moneymore, is an atmospheric "Ulster Planter" house built by William "Good-Will" Conyngham in 1680 as a wedding-gift for his wife, Anne Upton. The house can be visited and guided tours take visitors through the extensive library, a gun room, day nursery and a colourful costume collection displayed, rather appropriately, in the old laundry yard. The house also has its very own ghost. George Lenox Conyngham shot himself in 1816 after spending many months in a "very melancholy state of mind" and his grief-stricken wife Olivia has haunted the scene ever since. Her ghost is one of the most widely authenticated in Ireland.

Above: Part of the costume collection at Springhill.

The main road leads to Londonderry or Derry, also known as the "Maiden City." The name of the city gives a clue to its troubled past. It was founded by St. Columba in the middle of the sixth century and called "Doire", originally the place of the oaks. This was Anglicised into "Derry", but when the city was taken over during the seventeenth-century Ulster Plantation, its name became "Londonderry", thus reflecting the influence of the London finance companies which played a major part in this historic development.

Above: The Free Wall in the Bogside.

Right: The city walls overlooking Guildhall Square.

As a result the city's Irish nationalists call it "Derry" while the minority Unionists insist on "Londonderry." More recently the Council officially named it "Derry" but each local community continues to use its own name for their shared city. One of the best commentaries on this historical anachronism came from the local broadcaster and wit Gerry Anderson who christened it "Stroke City".

Derry has had many characters, in many generations. A well-known cleric in the seventeenth-eighteenth centuries was the Dean of Derry, Dr George Berkeley, who suggested that everything exists only in the all-seeing mind of God and was regarded by his peers either as a visionary or an eccentric.

Another eighteenth-century character born in Derry was Sir James Murray, an outstanding chemist who had a distinguished medical career in Dublin and Belfast. He devised a method of converting solid magnesia into a liquid form, which became the prototype of a modern production for indigestion. Murray was also the first to discover and to manufacture super-phosphates, which have been used for many years in the farming industry. He also warned, in 1849, about the harmful effects of electricity on health and recommended that homes and buildings should be insulated. This theory was discredited for many years, but recently doubts have been raised about the harmful effects of electro-magnetic radiation, particularly from mobile phones and masts. Perhaps Murray, like Berkeley, was ahead of his time.

Derry has been historically a barometer of Irish history—from the Catholic Jacobite Siege of 1689 which was successfully resisted by its Protestant Williamite citizens, right through to the Civil Rights marches of the late 1960s. The modern city retains its unique atmosphere where the past is still so much identified with the present.

One of Derry's greatest tourist attractions are the famous city Walls, among the best-preserved in Europe. They were completed in 1618, and rise to a height of 26 feet, and in places to a width of 30 feet. They were built to defend the new Plantation city from the Irish chieftains, and during the siege of 1689 they were resolutely defended by some 20,000 inhabitants, although around 7,000 died from hunger or disease. Many of the survivors lived "chiefly on starch made with tallow." A menu dating from the worst days of the Siege reveals that a dog cost 2/6d, a cat (obviously more of a delicacy) cost 4/6, while a rat cost 1/-. For the really hard-up, a mouse cost sixpence!

Above: St Columb's Church of Ireland Cathedral.
Left: The historic Guildhall.

artefacts, and in the Chapter House are many relics from the seventeenth-century Siege. These include a set of drums owned by the Hamilton Flute Band which joined the British Army en bloc during the First World War, with its indescribable carnage and blood-sacrifice, and claimed the lives of many Ulstermen, and others from different parts of Ireland.

The Cathedral also has many reminders of the peace and fulfillment of the Christian way of life, including a memorial window to Mrs Cecil Francis Alexander, the wife of a former Bishop of Derry. She is best-remembered for the famous hymns—*There is a Green Hill Far Away*, and *Once in Royal David's City*, as well as the lesser-known *The Golden Gates Are Lifted Up.*

Across the city is St. Eugene's Roman Catholic Cathedral, situated near the Bogside with the famous mural "You are now entering Free Derry". St. Eugene's, like its Protestant counterpart, is set on a hill as one of the twin pillars of Christendom in the city. St Eugene's was completed in 1873, and it is an ornate and attractive building with magnificent stained-glass. It is sobering to reflect on so many generations of Catholics and Protestants worshipping the same God in their different ways. Today, after so much of the pain of history, some of the wounds are beginning to heal, but this will take time.

When the Siege was broken there was great rejoicing, and even today the Apprentice Boys of Derry regularly take to the streets in orderly fashion to commemorate what they regard to be the Loyalist heroism of those days. Derry's Walls also withstood another major 20-week siege in 1649 when the city held at bay the Royalist forces during the English Civil War. Having successfully endured two major sieges, there are no prizes for guessing why Derry is called "the Maiden City."

Derry's rich history is also reflected in its churches. The Church of Ireland St. Columb's Cathedral was completed in 1633 in the "Planters' Gothic" style, and was the first in the British Isles to be established after the Reformation. However, in typically contrary fashion, it was named St. Columb's, after the Irish saint. The Cathedral has many historical

Guildhall Square is dominated by a fine building dating from 1890, and named in honour of the London Guilds. Despite a catastrophic fire in 1908 which destroyed the building, a new Guildhall was created in neo-Gothic style and sits in the square of the same name. The Guildhall was damaged by a bomb-blast during the troubles in 1972, but it was beautifully restored, and today it retains its impressive air as a symbol of this historic city.

The award-winning Tower Museum and Craft Village, just inside the Walls, provide access to a rich heritage and also quality shopping and local craft-work, while the large Richmond Shopping Centre on Shipquay Street provides a wide choice of merchandise. Those shoppers, or perhaps the husbands of shoppers, who require rest and recreation after contemplating their bank balances, might sample a quiet pint across the road in the River Inn, the site of the city's oldest sited bar, dating from 1684.

Above: Modern-day replica tower built on the original site of O'Doherty's Fort.

Above: An exhibit at the Tower Museum.

Above: The Craft Village.

Just outside the Walls, is the award-winning Millennium Forum, with a first-class concert and exhibition centre which underlines the city's rich musical and cultural heritage. It is said, rightly, that everyone in Derry can sing or play a musical instrument—or both—and the city has produced many famous entertainers including the celebrated tenor, the late Josef Locke, the internationally-acclaimed songwriter Phil Coulter, jazz musician Gay McIntyre, and many others—not least the plethora of Showbands which dominated the entertainment and ballroom life of Ireland in the late Fifties and Sixties.

Another attraction in the area is the Earhart Centre and Wildlife Sanctuary at Ballyarnett, just a mile beyond the landmark Foyle Bridge—a magnificent feat of engineering which provides a major gateway to Donegal. The centre contains an exhibition in memory of Amelia Earhart, the first woman to fly the Atlantic solo in 1932, and who landed in a field at Ballyarnett after a 15-hour flight and with an almost empty fuel tank. This is perhaps another dimension to the often-heard term "The Relief of Derry."

A visit to modern Derry is stimulating and refreshing, and an assurance that light can indeed come out of darkness. There has been a Renaissance in Derry since the grim days of the Troubles when the city was enveloped by fear and violence. Today there is an optimism about the place, and the relative peace and prosperity of the modern city may augur well for the future of the island as a whole. The visitor who is moving on from Derry towards the attractions of Tyrone can do so with a jaunty step, and the real hope that the worst of the past is now firmly where it should remain—in the past.

Bellaghy dates back to the seventeenth century and was built as part of the Plantation of Londonderry by the Vintners Company of London. They hoped to call the new village Vintnerstown but the old name persisted. It has been said that the original 12 houses were pre-fabricated in England and shipped over and then assembled on site. Bellaghy Bawn was built as protection for the English settlers against raids and was a square enclosed courtyard surrounded by walls and with two flanker towers set at diagonal corners. The bawn was destroyed in 1641 in a raid but was later rebuilt in 1643. A new house was then built on the site in the eighteenth century.

Bellaghy was also home to a young Seamus Heaney who later went on to win the Nobel Prize for Literature. One of the remaining towers of the bawn contains a library devoted to him and a schoolbag from his Anahorish Primary School days is on display to inspire Bellaghy's future poets.

Above: Bellaghy Bawn.

Chapter 4

On the Frontier-
Tyrone & Fermanagh

"There are strange things done in the midnight sun
By the men who moil for gold;
The Arctic trails have their secret tales
That would make your blood run cold"

Robert Service

Left: Devenish Island on Lower Lough Erne.

Above: Celtic Idol on Boa Island.

These lines from *The Cremation of Sam McGee* conjure up images of life on the north-west frontier in America which are redolent of the rugged yet beautiful north and west territory of Tyrone and Fermanagh with its bushes and lakelands, and also of the pioneering spirit of many of its people who left Ulster to seek a better life in the New World. Today its warm-hearted people are no less resilient and pioneering, and have kept alive an entrepreneurial and pioneering spirit in an area of Northern Ireland which experienced some of the worst of the recent Troubles.

The road from Derry follows the meanders of the River Foyle through attractive countryside, and on to the border town of Strabane, just a bridge across from Lifford in Co. Donegal. The history of this area has been inextricably entwined with the concept of "frontiers", not only with the Irish Republic but also overseas, and some of its early citizens played important roles in the burgeoning growth of the United States of America.

One of the main attractions of Strabane is a museum centred around Gray's Printing Shop at 49, Main Street. This is where John Dunlap was an apprentice in the eighteenth century, when the town was an important publishing and printing centre.

Dunlap emigrated to America, and in 1776 he would be asked to print the American Declaration of Independence in the broadsheets used to inform the world of the newly independent America. A few days later he cannily replicated the information on the front of his own newspaper, *The Pennsylvania Packet*, which would later grow into America's first daily newspaper.

It is believed that the first newspaper outside America to print the Declaration was the Belfast *News Letter*. It received the text which arrived by boat in Londonderry only six weeks after it was signed. This would have been a European "scoop" of the first magnitude, with Ulster people reading about it in August 1776 before King George III

himself in London was able to do so. Seven of the 56 signatories of the Declaration of Independence were Scots-Irish. It was drafted by Thomas Jefferson and transcribed by Charles Thomson, who originated from Maghera.

James Wilson was also an apprentice at Gray's Printing Shop and he moved to the States as well, just five years before Dunlap died in 1812. He married a Sion Mills girl whom he had met on the emigrant ship, and later became the editor of a Philadelphia newspaper. Their grandson Woodrow Wilson was President of the United States from 1913-1921, and the Wilson ancestral home at Dergalt is now open to the public. Incidentally, three other US Presidents came from families who lived west of the Bann—James K. Polk, James Buchanan and Ulysses Simpson Grant.

South of Strabane on the main road to Newtownstewart is Sion Mills, a neat village which owes its development to the textile trade. The God-fearing Herdman family created a model linen village not dissimilar to that of the Richardsons in Bessbrook, Co. Armagh in the middle of the nineteenth century. Sion Mills still retains its charm, and it has several fine churches, as befits a village founded on Christian principles.

Above: Gray's Printing Shop where Dunlap and Wilson learned their trade.
Right: Scenic Glenelly Valley from the air.

A famous newspaper story relates how a funeral tribute to a local worthy became garbled by the time it was printed in a Belfast newspaper. Instead of being described as "a watcher on Zion's Hill" he was referred to as "a watchman in Sion Mills." Some of Sion Mills' most enduring headlines were made on a historic day in 1969 when the local cricket team scuttled out the famous West Indies side on the local pitch.

The town of Newtownstewart, further south, found itself in the headlines for the wrong reasons in the mid-nineteenth century when a bank cashier was murdered and robbed of the then large amount of £1,600. The local police chief, District Inspector Montgomery of the Royal Irish Constabulary, led the hunt in the wrong direction, for the very good reason that he had killed the bank-clerk and hidden the money in a quarry.

However the long arm of the law, and perhaps divine intervention, ensured that justice was done when floodwater in the quarry exposed the missing money, and the murderer was found out. Newtownstewart today has no such headlines, and continues its quiet rural existence amid some of the best fishing country in Ireland.

A few miles west of Newtownstewart is Castlederg, the ancestral base of the noted American frontiersman Davy Crockett, whose last stand at the Battle of the Alamo has been regaled to later generations in word and song. Crockett was part of the generations of Scots-Irish who made such a remarkable contribution to American frontier history,

with their grit, fighting prowess and fundamental Christian faith, as well as their talent for making music and illicit mountain brew! The story of their contribution, and that of others, is well told in the excellent Ulster-American Folk Park, a few miles north of Omagh, which opened in 1976.

This historical complex is based around the ancestral homestead of Judge Thomas Mellon who was born at Camphill in 1813, and emigrated with his parents to Pennsylvania where he later founded a large industrial empire.

In his autobiography Mellon emphasised the virtues of hard work, temperance, caution and sober living—"I have never seen a horse race or a boat race, or played a game of cards in my life, or incurred any extra hazardous risks—never speculating in property of any kind without I saw a sure thing in it."

The Ulster-American Folk Park is fortunately rather more entertaining, and its exhibitions emphasise the different waves of Ulster emigration which contributed so much to America. The Old World outlines the first mass movement beginning around 1717 which took thousands of Ulster families to the virgin land of the ever-expanding frontier. The New World focuses on the immigration which reached its peak in the second half of the nineteenth century, and which brought an exodus of people from all over Ireland where they settled for the most part in the growing cities of America.

There are a number of fascinating exhibits which range from a small log cabin of the type first used by the Mellons in Western Pennsylvania, to the boyhood home of John Joseph Hughes, who left nearby Augher for America. He later became Archbishop of New York, and helped to build the magnificent St. Patrick's Cathedral on Fifth Avenue.

All of this, and much more, is featured in the Folk Park which is unmissable for anyone who has literally a passing or a much deeper interest in the enduring links between Northern Ireland and the USA.

Above: A wagon on display at the Ulster-American Folk Park.
Left: The ancestral home of the industrious Judge Thomas Mellon.

Each September the Folk Park stages an important "Bluegrass" festival featuring the music of the Smokey Mountains and the Appalachians of Tennessee. The Scots-Irish settlers brought with them their music, which has strongly influenced the country and folk music of America. Two of the best-known modern exponents have been Dolly Parton and Jimmy Rodgers.

Not far from the Ulster-American Folk Park is Gortin Glen Forest Park which, appropriately, has an American tree trail and other attractions including one of the best scenic drives in the county.

On the B48 road down to Omagh there is the Ulster History Park, which features early Ulster settlements and covers some 9,000 years of history. At the time of writing, however, it is closed but it is hoped that this will prove only a temporary measure.

Omagh is a bustling rural town with a sturdy spirit. It is still coming to terms with a dreadful terrorist bombing several years ago which killed 29 people, injured many others, and devastated the town and the entire country. Today Omagh goes about its business with quiet stoicism, and there is now a beautiful memorial park in the town, but the wounds run deep. Its people are friendly and hard-working, and its literary sons include the writers Brian Friel and Benedict Kiely, as well as the song-writer Jimmy Kennedy who is also closely associated with Portstewart.

One of the most notable buildings in Omagh is the late nineteenth-century Sacred Heart Catholic Church, with unequal spires, and is thought to have been modelled on Chartres Cathedral in France. The Courthouse built on classical lines at the top of the main street is also impressive.

The main road to Enniskillen and the Fermanagh lakelands runs past the Clanabogan Camphill Community, one of several communities in Northern Ireland for people with special needs. The others are at Glencraig and Holywood in Co. Down and at Mourne Grange, Kilkeel. These are part of the world-wide Camphill movement, established on the principles of Rudolf Steiner more than sixty years ago.

At the village of Irvinestown the Lady of the Lake Festival takes place each summer and recently an international equestrian centre opened at Necarne Castle nearby. The summer festival owes its origin to a legend about a lady clad in flowing garments and carrying beautiful flowers. She was said to have travelled in the mists between the nearby islands of Lough Erne and the shore. Tradition claimed that a sighting of her was a good omen.

At Irvinestown the road forks, and beyond Kesh, well-known for its boat-building, the A35 passes through the beautiful scenery of Lower Lough Erne to Belleek. Castle Archdale, to the south of Kesh, was one of the most important military bases on Lough Erne which, like Derry, played a vital role in the Battle of the Atlantic during the Second World War. Various centres around the Lough were occupied by Allied personnel, and the Belfast-built Sunderland and American Catalina flying-boats were based at Killadeas and Castle Archdale. Near the village of Garrison on the shores of Lough Melvin, a radio beacon was installed and its beam was so strong that it reached Gander in Newfoundland— a considerable technological feat in those days.

Traces remain of these installations and bases, and they still attract war veterans and military historians. At Castle Archdale a Country Caravan Park is situated on the site of the former aircraft hangars, and there is a small museum dedicated to the war-time operators. According to a local story, the military authorities had difficulty with the construction of a wartime runway at St. Angelo, near Enniskillen. Workmen were reluctant to move a fairy thorn tree for fear of incurring a traditional Irish curse. Finally two men were persuaded to move the bush, but one later met with an untimely death. The power of Irish folk-lore runs deep. St. Angelo is now a small civil airport.

Belleek is the most westerly point of the United Kingdom, right on the border with the Irish Republic. The Belleek Pottery is world-famous for its distinctive china, and has been in existence since 1857 when the first products were made from locally-obtained feldspar, which now comes from Scandinavia. Each item is hand-decorated requiring a high degree of skill and individual artistry. For example, each petal in a floral design or a twist in a basket display has its own

Above: A wild deer in Gortin Country Park.

Right: Gortin Lakes from the air.

character, and the finishing skill is handed down from generation to generation. Belleek china is highly-prized as a collector's item, and it is particularly sought-after in the United States.

The A46 road from Belleek reaches Lough Navar viewpoint, and although it requires concentrated driving to get there, the truly magnificent view over Lower Lough Erne makes the effort worthwhile.

To the east are the still noteworthy ruins of the early seventeenth-century Tully Castle, while further along near the lough shore is Ely Lodge, the Fermanagh seat of the Duke of Westminster, one of the richest men in the United Kingdom.

An earlier house once stood on this site but unbelievably was blown up in 1870 by its owner, the 4th Marquess of Ely, to celebrate his twenty-first birthday! He had planned to build a new house on the site but in the event he failed to do so, spending most of the time at his Wexford home.

In this area of Lower Lough there are also the remains of the once very desirable property of the early seventeenth-century Monea Castle, one of the best preserved in Fermanagh. It was built around 1618 and has impressive barrel towers. The original owner was the Rector of Devenish, the Reverend Malcolm Hamilton, and the castle's design reflects his Scottish roots. The castle was destroyed by a fire in the mid-eighteenth century and was abandoned. The well-preserved ruins remain, overlooking a lake and are approached by a avenue of beech trees.

An alternative and circuitous though beautiful route to Enniskillen is through Derrygonnelly where the visitor can enjoy local hospitality and some fine Irish traditional music. Further west, the village of Garrison is at the edge of Lough Melvin which, like all the Fermanagh lakes, is an angler's paradise, and it has early salmon and three distinctive species of trout.

The B52 road then leads south past Upper and Lower Lough MacNean, with Belcoo sitting neatly between the two. It is worth seeking on the map the Marlbank Loop, a scenic drive which affords outstanding views of Lower Lough MacNean. However the main tourist attraction in this area is the Marble Arch Caves, a vast complex of underground lakes, rivers, waterfalls and other glories of nature. These were created by the erosion of millions of tons of limestone by acid rivers and streams draining from the northern slopes of the Cuilcagh Mountains.

Once the haunt mainly of pot-holers and other hardy souls, the Marble Arch Caves have been well-developed as a major tourist attraction. One of the highlights of a visit is the boat trip along the subterranean waters, though the Caves may be closed for security reasons due to heavy rainfall. Potential visitors should check in advance.

Above: Early seventeenth-century Monea Castle.

Left: The angler's paradise of Lough Melvin.

Next Page: A boat trip in the Marble Arch Caves.

The other major attraction in this area is the stately home Florence Court, which is now in the care of the National Trust.

One of the most important houses in Ulster, it was built in the mid-eighteenth century by John Cole, father of the first Earl of Enniskillen. It is particularly noted for its rococo plasterwork by Robert West of Dublin. The furnishings include travelling chests which belonged to King William III and Queen Mary, as well as a chamber-pot with the features of William Ewart Gladstone inside. He was the nineteenth-century British Prime Minister who strongly advocated Home Rule for Ireland, and the Unionists in Fermanagh left him in no doubt about what they thought of him.

Florence Court has a superb setting, and its surrounding woodlands contain the progenitor of the world-famous "Irish Yew", which was discovered on the estate as a seedling by the head gardener in the late 1700s. It cannot be truly reproduced by seed, and has to be propagated from cuttings. The visitor could usefully spend a day exploring the delights of Florence Court and the Marble Arch Caves nearby.

Enniskillen, the main town in Fermanagh, has its own history and dignity in its setting on an island between Upper and Lower Lough Erne. It was the seat of the Maguires, the local chieftains, and the home of famous regiments including the Royal Inniskilling Fusiliers and the Inniskilling Dragoons. The Duke of Wellington remarked that the Inniskillings saved the centre of his line at Waterloo. Napoleon reflected ruefully "That regiment with the castle on their caps—they know not when they are beaten."

Enniskillen has a colourful history, and the former pupils of the Portora Royal School, founded by King James I in 1608, include the writers Oscar Wilde and Samuel Beckett, as well as Henry Francis Lyte who wrote a number of popular hymns including *Abide With Me*. Well-known recent citizens included the pianist and composer Valerie Trimble, whose family owned the splendidly-named newspaper *The Impartial Reporter*, though not quite so famous as the now defunct *Skibbereen Eagle* in the Irish Republic which warned the world that it had its eye on the Czar of Russia.

Left: Florence Court, built in the mid-eighteenth century.

Enniskillen, like Omagh, was the scene of one of the worst atrocities in the recent Troubles when eleven people died and others were badly injured in a no-warning terrorist bomb which was detonated at the local Cenotaph on Remembrance Sunday in 1987. A local draper, Senator Gordon Wilson was caught in the blast that killed his daughter Marie, a student nurse. Later that day he said in a broadcast that he bore no ill will towards her killers, and his words of forgiveness made a huge impression around the world.

Today the local Cenotaph also contains the names of those who died in the blast, and a new building erected in 2001 by the University of Ulster stands at the scene of the explosion. The Clinton Centre was opened by the former President of the United States, Bill Clinton, and was built to focus on peace-building in Northern Ireland and overseas. Enniskillen and its people have shown resilience, and look for better days ahead but, like Omagh, the sadness remains.

On the way north from Enniskillen is another superb stately home— Castle Coole—which is also in the care of the National Trust. Set in its own grounds away from the main road, this late eighteenth-century building on a mid-seventeenth century site has a most striking Palladian front of Portland stone, and it is equally breath-taking inside. It was recently restored to its original grandeur, and like Florence Court ought not to be missed. There are pleasant walks in the surrounding estate, and a lake with a large colony of greylag geese whose forebears at successive stages have been in residence for almost three centuries.

Not far from Castle Coole is the modern Ardhowen Theatre which provides year-round entertainment in a delightful setting near the lough shore. Of special interest are the Enniskillen Drama Festival held each March and a Summer Drama Festival from June to August.

Enniskillen Castle dates back to the early fifteenth century when the original castle on the site was built by Hugh Maguire. His family had secured the whole of the Erne basin and by 1484 the castle would be the family stronghold. The castle was of strategic importance and over the years it was captured and then retaken many times by the O'Neills, O'Donnells and even the English until it was finally wrecked by Niall O'Donnell in 1602. The castle was rebuilt in 1607 by the planter William Cole as a fortified house with a curtain wall and flanker towers and became the centre of the new Plantation town, "Inniskilling." The garrison town rallied to the Williamite cause and in 1688 managed to prevent a large Irish force from joining the siege at Derry. The castle continued to house troops until the 1950s and is now home to the regimental museum of the Royal Inniskilling Fusiliers.

Above: The impressive exterior of Enniskillen Castle.

Above: Castle Coole, also in the care of the National Trust.

Left: The drawing-room at Florence Court.

THE LAKELANDS

Some people believe that the Antrim Coast is the crown of Ulster's varied and beautiful scenery, but the brightest jewel is undoubtedly the Fermanagh Lakeland and Upper Lough Erne which have between them more than 150 islands, and many of them are worth exploring. However, the visitor would do well to hire a boat, and a wide range of watercraft is available from the most modern motor-cruisers to much smaller craft.

Boating and fishing are the main tourist attractions of this beautiful area, and the annual international angling competition held in May attracts a large number of fishermen from the British Isles and continental Europe. The traditional tall stories in local pubs and restaurants about the day's fishing require little embellishment, as the catches from Lough Erne in quantity and size are often record-breaking in themselves.

With the comparatively recent opening of the waterways it is now possible to navigate by motor-cruiser for some 500 miles from Belleek on Lower Lough Erne to the Shannon estuary deep in the Irish Republic. This is an ideal way to relax for those who prefer a more leisurely holiday with frequent changes of beautiful scenery. A number of hire-cruise operators are based in the Fermanagh Lakeland, and the basic skills of messing about in boats safely are not as difficult to pick up as they might at first appear.

For those who want to spend time around Lower Lough Erne the lakelands have much of interest—from the romantically-named Boa Island with its ancient graveyard and two-faced statue of a Celtic idol, to the ruins of a sixth-century monastery founded by St Ninnid on Inishmacsaint island. A fourteen-foot high cross dating from the tenth century can still be seen there.

On White Island there are seven ancient Christian stone figures which seem to give more than a passing nod to the old Celtic beliefs. Carved of stone and placed against the walls of a now roofless twelfth-century church the statues show a grinning sheela-na-gig (an ancient female fertility symbol), a man holding two griffins by the scruff of their necks and a man with a shield, sword and brooch. On a more religious theme the other statues show an abbot complete with crozier and bell, a priestly figure scratching his chin and a seated man with a book. A seventh figure is incomplete, and one cannot help wondering why it wasn't finished.

Devenish Island is the largest island in Lower Lough Erne and probably the best known. St Molaise founded a monastery here in the sixth century, and the site was once one of the most important centres of Christian learning in Ireland with many students attached to the monastery. The Vikings knew of its importance and raided the site in both the ninth and twelfth centuries. The round tower was built in the

Above: Stone figures on White Island.

Right: The round tower on Devenish Island.

Next Page: Sunset on Lough Erne from Lough Navar Forest.

twelfth century as a refuge for the be-leaguered monks. They would grab what they could from the tiny church, climb the ladder, bring it inside and wait until the raiders had gone. Visitors can still climb the tower and look out over the extensive and well-preserved remains of an early medieval Christian settlement, and the ruins of a priory abandoned after the dissolution of the monasteries in 1603.

In one of the ancient buildings there is a ninth-century poem attributed to St. Manchen and later translated from the Gaelic by the Irish writer Frank O'Connor. It is a poem about peace, both externally and internally, and the best of the Lakeland atmosphere is well summarised.

Above: Lower Lough Erne in the morning.

Upper Lough Erne is less deep than its lower cousin and the shallow waters and islands found there are a peaceful haven for wild birds and even wild goats. Most of the islands are too small for people to live on now but some were inhabited, and the remains of cottages and even mansions can still be visited by boat. One mansion dating from 1840s on Inishrath has even been converted into a Hindu temple by the Hare Krishna group who now live there.

Although the islands in the Upper Lough are peaceful now it wasn't always so and one headland stretching out into the lake is home to the ruins of Old Crom Castle. Built by the Scottish planter, Michael Balfour, in 1611 the castle was enlarged with a bawn in 1629 and was later acquired by the Crichton family, ancestors of the Earls of Erne. The castle withstood two ferocious sieges in 1689 during the Jacobite Rising and was lucky to survive. Sadly, the castle was destroyed in an accidental fire in 1764 and was abandoned by the Crichton family who built a new castellated mansion nearby, the New Crom Castle. The vast Crom Estate is now in the care of the National Trust and can be visited from April to September, although the castle itself is private.

Above: Cruisers at Castle Archdale.

Left: New Crom Castle. The estate is now in the care of the National Trust.

The Fermanagh Lakeland is not just a place. It's an attitude of mind.

The road winds to the north and back to County Tyrone along the historic Clogher Valley with the poetically-named villages of Fivemiletown, Clogher and Augher. It is said that a former inhabitant of Augher Castle kept a large supply of shillelaghs and handed these to opposing parties in a lawsuit. He hoped that this would enable them to settle the case in their own way.

Above: The rebuilt ancestral home of 18th US President Ulysses Simpson Grant.

Right: Augher Castle in the Clogher Valley.

Near Augher is the historic Knockmany Hill with a passage grave and patterns similar to those at Newgrange. In Clogher there is St. Macartin's Church of Ireland Cathedral, and Fivemiletown has an early eighteenth-century parish church. Near Fivemiletown is the ancestral territory of Field-Marshall Lord Alanbrooke, a distinguished British soldier, and also of Lord Brookeborough, the Prime Minister of Northern Ireland from 1943-63.

At Caledon is the Castle home of the local Earl, and the birth-place of the former Field-Marshall Alexander of Tunis, who was considered by Sir Winston Churchill as one of his finest commanders in the Second World War. After the War he became a well-regarded Governor-General of Canada, and also was appointed Minister of Defence in Churchill's Government. The village of Caledon itself has a distinct rural charm, and just outside the Caledon Estate the restoration of the Workers' Houses has been completed.

One of the most interesting historic developments in this area was the Clogher Valley Railway which operated from 1887 to 1941. It was 37 miles long and linked villages and towns between Tynan and Maguiresbridge. This was a rare form of transport, even by Irish standards, and it ran along village main streets. Some of the original stations can still be seen along the route.

A local historian Dr G. Gillespie outlined some of the eccentricities of the railway in a leaflet published by the Clogher Valley Tourist Development Association. He noted that the locomotives had "a cow-catcher," and an immense and ornate oil lamp, later replaced by electricity. Instead of a whistle they had a hooter of the type associated with harbour tug-boats—it hiccuped a few times before producing a most mournful wail. He recalls, "We said 'She's blowing', and I have nostalgic memories of the late train hooting its sad way down the valley on frosty winter nights."

At the end of the Clogher Valley near Ballygawley is the rebuilt ancestral home of the 18th United States President Ulysses Simpson Grant, and also a visitor centre. In 1878 the President returned to Ulster to receive the freedom of Londonderry, and stopped off at his ancestral homestead. Ballygawley once had a thriving linen business, a distillery, a glove factory and large cattle fairs. Today it is much more sedate, having been by-passed by the main road, no doubt to the relief of the local residents.

Cookstown is famous for having one of the widest and longest main streets in Ireland and the street was part of an ambitious plan to build a model town by an eighteenth-century Tyrone landlord, William Stewart, which never quite got on the ground. His descendants had more success with their building plans and enlisted John Nash, the famous English architect, to build Killymoon Castle. The parklands surrounding the castle are now a popular golf course.

Ardboe Cross stands on the windswept shores of Lough Neagh on an early monastic site, ten miles from Cookstown. Standing at over eighteen feet and dating back to the tenth century, the east and west sides are covered in twenty-two panels depicting Old and New Testament scenes. An old graveyard nearby contains the Ardboe Pin Tree. Believers hoping for a cure would hammer a pin or coin into the bark of the beech tree with prayers for restored health. But those eager to prise out the coins or pins should remember that the disease the sufferer hoped to cure was also said to come out with the coin!

Loughry Manor, outside Cookstown is famous for its agricultural college but the plantation mansion's history stretches back to the eighteenth century and one famous guest was Jonathan Swift. A close friend of the owner Robert Lindsay, he stayed in 1722 during the period he was writing *Gulliver's Travels*. Portraits of Stella and Vanessa, his friends and companions, hang in the Old Library.

Dungannon, further south, is home to Tyrone Crystal and visitors flock to see the beautiful glassware being made by hand. The craft first came to Dungannon in 1771 with a small group of Bristol glassmakers. The skills died out but were eventually revived in 1971 by Father Austin Eustace who wanted to provide work for his community. The crystal is exported worldwide and is one of the success stories in the region.

Leaving the counties of Fermanagh and Tyrone the road leads to another site of interest to—Armagh—the ecclesiastical capital of Ireland, and the heart of the Orchard County. This is indubitably the territory of St. Patrick, the Patron Saint of Ireland who left his mark on the city and its people. County Armagh has its own character, like each of the counties of Northern Ireland, and also its own attractions, starting with its capital city Armagh.

Beaghmore Stone Circles date back to the Bronze Age and were uncovered during peat-cutting in the 1930s. The significance of the seven stone circles and dozen or so alignments has been lost in time but similar circles and lines have been found in other parts of the Sperrins.

Above: Beaghmore Stone Circles in the Sperrins.

Left: Ardboe Cross on the shores of Lough Neagh.

Chapter 5

Armagh and the 'Orchard County'.

"It was most necessary to spread our nets so that a great multitude and throng might be caught for God, and that there be clerics everywhere to baptize and exhort a people in need and want."

St. Patrick from his *Confessio*

Left: Spring blossom in the Armagh Orchards.

Above: St Patrick's Roman Catholic Cathedral.

These autobiographical words are from Patrick, Ireland's patron saint who established his main church in Armagh in 445 AD, and thereby gave this charming city the right to describe itself as "the ecclesiastical capital of Ireland." It is a mantle which it wears today with dignity, and it combines the best of the present with the highlights of the past on which it builds its reputation and main attractions.

Armagh is an essential stopping place for any visitor who wishes to find out more about the long history of Christianity in Ireland and how it has affected the politics and community life of the entire island.

While there is no doubt that this is "St. Patrick's City", with the two great Cathedrals in his name—Church of Ireland and Roman Catholic—dominating the skyline, Armagh has much else to savour and enjoy. These include its classically Georgian buildings, its wide and eye-catching Mall, the Observatory and Planetarium, other churches, museums and modern tourist attractions such as the Palace Stables Heritage Centre.

In all of this, the story of two men dominates the colourful and often disturbed history of Armagh—St. Patrick himself, and also Richard Robinson, later Lord Rokeby. He was a wealthy eighteenth-century Church of Ireland Primate who was Archbishop from 1765 to 1795 and who set out to make Armagh architecturally and educationally worthy of its title as the ecclesiastical capital of Ireland. The heritage stemming from the mission of these two exceptional Christians more than 1,300 years apart is evident all over the city.

Down the centuries it has had countless visitors, quite a few hostile but the majority friendly. In recent years friendly visitors have included important politicians such as the former US President Bill Clinton and his wife Senator Hillary Clinton, British Prime Ministers John Major and Tony Blair, Irish Presidents Mary Robinson and Mary McAleese, and the former

President of the European Union Jacques Delors. There is still much speculation about the origins of Armagh's most distinguished visitor of all, St. Patrick, and the precise details of his mission to Ireland. Indeed there is so much speculation that it is difficult to sift the facts from the fiction.

Scholars disagree about Patrick's origins and his work as a missionary. Some commentators claim that there may have been at least two Patricks, others believe that he never existed, and yet others suggest that he was confused with another missionary called Palladius who was briefly in Leinster within the broad framework of Patrick's lifetime. There is wide speculation about his original home, ranging from Kilpatrick in Scotland to Glastonbury near the south coast of England, but it is generally thought that the place of his capture was on the west coast of Roman Britain in a region that was subjected to incursions by raiders from Ireland. Nor is there any scholarly agreement about his place of servitude. Patrick himself mentions only one place-name "Silva Focluti", and the speculation ranges from Co. Mayo to Magherafelt, Strangford Lough and Faughal, near Cushendall. The most popular tradition suggests, however, that he worked as a slave at or near Slemish in Co. Antrim.

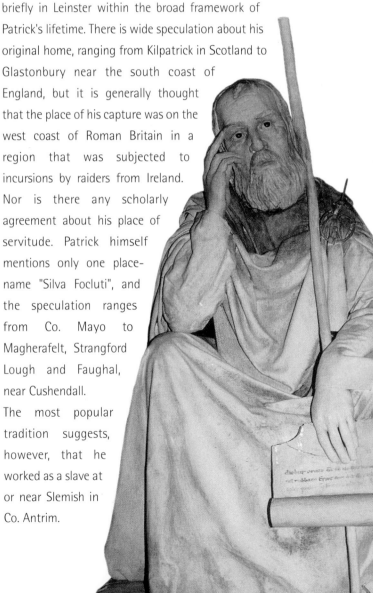

Right: Model of St. Patrick at the St Patrick's Trian.

Far Right: The Church of Ireland Cathedral.

One of the best scholarly authorities on Patrick was the late Bishop R.P.C. Hanson, formerly a Professor at the University of Manchester. He suggested that while there are no accurate dates about his life and work, Patrick was born about 390 AD, was kidnapped around 406 AD, that he escaped in 412 AD, that he returned to Ireland as a Bishop between 425 AD and 435 AD and that he died about 460 AD.

In fact the most reliable account of Patrick's life is contained in his autobiographical *Confessio* which was written in his old age and refers to his capture by Irish pirates, his service as a slave in Ireland, his dramatic escape and his return to the island as a Christian missionary. It is a dramatic story, written in rudimentary Latin, and its tone underlines the humble, unassuming nature of Patrick who was also a man of great courage and tenacity. He begins his *Confessio* with the words, "I am Patrick, a sinner, most unlearned, the least of all the faithful, and utterly despised by many."

However, it was the same Patrick whose mission led to the flowering of Irish Christianity and whose disciples in later ages travelled all over Europe to keep alive the light of Christianity in a dark world.

Patrick is a worthy saint of the Irish, even though many people associate him only with the somewhat "stage Irish" celebrations surrounding St. Patrick's Day. Those who wish to know more about this remarkable man should read his *Confessio*, and his earlier *Letter to Coroticus*, which is a scathing attack on a Welsh war-lord who abducted a large number of Patrick's young converts and carried them into a life of slavery. (The translation of Patrick's writings are available in most bookshops.)

The most confident assertion of Patrick's presence in Armagh is contained in the notice-board of the Church of Ireland Cathedral which states "Founded by the Saint 445 AD." Though there have been many versions of the Cathedral, this hill is regarded to be the site where Patrick founded his main church long ago. As if to further underline the

Above: Memorial to Brian Boru at the Church of Ireland Cathedral.

Left: St. Patrick's Roman Catholic Cathedral looks over the city of Armagh.

Cathedral's authenticity, inside the building there is a long, brown notice-board with gold lettering which names all the Abbots, Bishops and Archbishops of Armagh beginning with Patrick and ends with the current Primate, Archbishop Robin Eames, who was appointed in 1986.

On the outer wall of the Cathedral is another confirmation of its ancient history. A large plaque states "Near This Spot On the North Side Of The Church was laid the body of Brian Boroimhe Slain at Clontarf A.D. MXIV"—a reference to the High King of Ireland Brian Boru who had visited the Cathedral in the year 1004 and had placed 20 ounces of gold on the High Altar. Some ten years later he was victorious at the Battle of Clontarf but, tragically, he and his son and grandson all died in the fierce fight against the last of the Vikings in Ireland.

Today the Cathedral stands peacefully as one of the bastions of Irish history, although down the centuries it was damaged by many fires and by the incursions of invaders. It was struck by lightning in 995 AD and remained roofless for more than a century until Archbishop Celus re-roofed it with shingles in 1125. It suffered considerable damage in the sixteenth century, but after the Restoration of Charles II in 1660 Archbishop Margetson from 1663 continued the work of restoration and conserved the ruins of the old Cathedral which became the nucleus of the present Church. This was enhanced by a further restoration by Archbishop Robinson in 1765.

The last significant restoration occurred in 1834, and William Makepeace Thackeray on visiting the Cathedral in the 1840s described it as being "neat and trim like a lady's drawing-room. It wants a hundred years at least to cool the raw colour of the stones..." Thackeray also noted that the sermon at Morning Service lasted only 20 minutes and exclaimed, "Can this be Ireland?"

One of the most interesting Archbishops of Armagh was James Usher (1581-1656) who became famous as the man who dated the time of creation to 9.00am on Monday 23 October 4004 BC. This date was inserted into the margin of the Authorized bible until as late as the nineteenth century.

Another figure of great historical importance is the "Tandragee Man", a statue dating from the Iron Age around 1000 BC, which was found in a garden in Tandragee, near Armagh. In the Chapter Room is a stone carving of the mythological goddess Macha. The Cathedral also has a broken eleventh-century Market Cross, and in the south transept there is an impressive chapel to a locally recruited regiment the Royal Irish Fusiliers.

Outside the Cathedral, on the left facing towards the city, there is a fine sweep of houses named Vicar's Hill. These were originally for vicars'

Above: Vicar's Hill built for the widows of Church of Ireland vicars.
Right: St. Patrick's Roman Catholic Cathedral.

widows, and the end house No.11 is the birth-place of Sir Charles Wood, the noted nineteenth-twentieth century composer who died in 1926 and left a legacy of more than 250 sacred works, plus a large number of hymn tunes. He is commemorated each year by a Charles Wood Summer School.

One of the most beautiful buildings in Armagh is St. Patrick's Roman Catholic Cathedral, which sits high on a hill above the city and stares directly across the valley to its Church of Ireland counterpart. According to tradition, this is the hill where St. Patrick had carried a fawn on his shoulders to a "safe place", with the doe following.

The Cathedral was started in 1840, partly due to the drive of Archbishop William Crolly, who had negotiated the site with the Earl of Dartrey. Building stopped during the Irish famine, and even today the "Famine Line" can be seen in the completed building. There were many fund-raising events to help build the Cathedral, and much of the costs were contributed by local parishioners and supporters from all over the world. In 1865 there was a Grand Bazaar to raise funds, and prizes were donated by the then Pope and the Emperors of Austria and France. However a beautiful Dublin-made grandfather-clock still stands in the Cathedral Vestry as an unclaimed prize! The exterior of the building was finished and dedicated in 1873, but it was not until 1904 that the interior was completed and the Cathedral finally consecrated.

Just behind the Cathedral is the Tomas O'Fiaich Memorial Library and Archive with its fine Irish collections, and named after a much-loved recent Primate, Cardinal Tomas O'Fiaich. Another noteworthy building is St. Malachy's Chapel in Irish Street, which is named after the local man who became a pivotal twelfth-century Archbishop of Armagh, a confidant of the Pope and a friend of St. Bernard of Clairvaux.

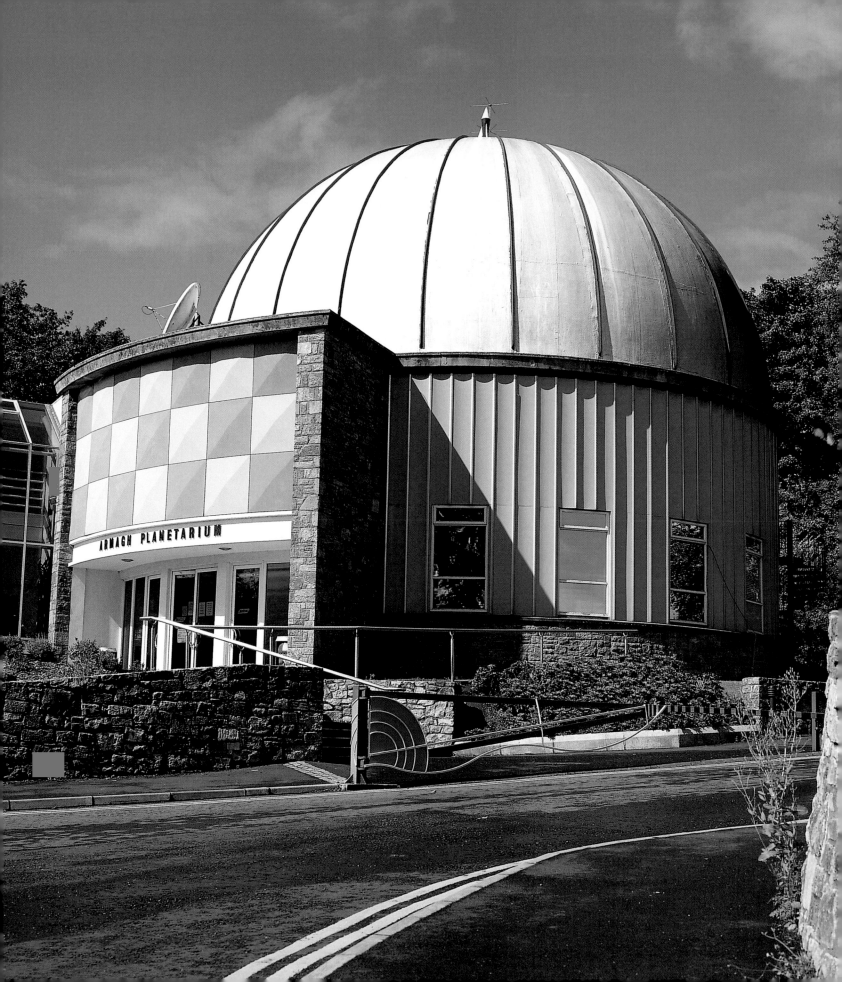

Armagh Public Library, envisaged in 1771 by Archbishop Robinson was established by an Act of Parliament two years later. It was the first public library in Ireland outside Dublin, and its correct title remains the "Armagh Public Library", and not the often-used term "the Robinson Library."

The recently restored Library contains a number of important historical artefacts, including a first edition of Dean Jonathan Swift's Gulliver's Travels.

In 1999, however, this was stolen by raiders who entered the Library, tied up a female assistant, and made off with a number of treasures, including two Corporation Maces dating from 1656. These were found in a bag lying near Dublin airport, and later two men were arrested and charged with handling stolen property. Fortunately the first two-volume edition of *Gulliver's Travels* was found by the Irish police and handed back for safe keeping.

Just beyond the Library is the handsome campus of the Queen's University at Armagh. A university in the city was part of the vision of Archbishop Robinson, but this did not become a reality until its launch in 1995—the sesquicentenary year of Queen's itself—and its later establishment in the old City Infirmary built by Robinson in 1774. The first graduates from Queen's received their parchments in July 2000.

Another noted institution in Armagh was part of Robinson's dream for a university city. He established an Observatory in 1789 which, he hoped, would provide a School of Sciences for his proposed university. This did not happen, but the Observatory established a high local, national and international reputation for its work on Astrophysics and associated sciences, including more recently the measures needed to combat the potential devastation of asteroids and comets impacting on planet Earth. The Observatory has many interesting historical scientific instruments including a telescope presented by Queen Victoria in 1840 that once belonged to George III.

The Observatory is also associated with the Armagh Planetarium which was founded in 1968 with a young Sir Patrick Moore of *Sky at*

Above: The Armagh Public Library.

Above: The Observatory founded by the visionary Archbishop Robinson.
Left: The more recent Planetarium which was founded in 1968.

Night fame as their first director. The Planetarium, which is essentially a shop-window for astronomy, was the first in Northern Ireland and was also one of the first in the United Kingdom. The Planetarium is visitor-based, and an important part of its work is to be pro-active and to reach out to the community and to develop children's interest in science.

Above: The Royal School Armagh which the Duke of Wellington once attended.

Across the road from the Observatory and Planetarium is The Royal School Armagh, which traces its origins back to 1608.

Its more famous former pupils include a young Arthur Wellesley, now better known as the Duke of Wellington, who so famously defeated Napoleon in 1815 and later became British Prime Minister, and his older brother Richard who was twice Lord-Lieutenant of Ireland and Governor-General of India. Both attended the school for varying lengths of time in the 1770s. Isaac Corry, the Speaker of the Irish Parliament, and Lord Castlereagh, British Foreign Secretary at the time of the Battle of Waterloo also attended. In 1986 The Royal School amalgamated with Armagh Girls' High School, which had been founded as a private school in Russell Street in the early twentieth century.

Back in the centre of Armagh is the splendid Mall, which in Archbishop Robinson's time was known as "The Common", with a surrounding race-course. In 1773 Robinson had the race-course removed, and The Common was leased to the city to provide a public park. It was gradually developed into an elegant area surrounded by some of Armagh's best classical architecture, including the Courthouse, the County Museum, which was once the County Gaol, and the Royal Irish Fusiliers Museum. The forerunners of this ancient regiment, itself a part of history, were the "Eagle Takers", the first group to capture one of Napoleon's Imperial Eagle Standards in 1811. The Museum also tells the story of the Armagh, Cavan and Monaghan Militias.

On a spring or summer afternoon Armagh has the ambience of an English county town when the local cricket club takes to the pitch along the centre of the Mall. Armagh is a noted sporting centre, with a championship Gaelic football team which won the 2002 All-Ireland

Above: Armagh County Museum which formerly housed the County Gaol.
Right: Autumn leaves in the Mall at Armagh.

Final and were runners-up to neighbouring Tyrone the next year. Significantly, this was the first time that two Ulster clubs contested the All-Ireland final. Armagh also has a good golf club and flourishing hockey clubs, as well as its own indigenous sport of Road Bowls. This is played with a 28-ounce solid iron ball, which is bowled along a selected path of open roadway. The winner is the player to reach the finishing line in the least number of throws or shots.

Armagh is so steeped in history that the visitor on the Pilgrim's Path would do well to pause in the St. Patrick's Trian, where there is a comprehensive exhibition on the life and work of St. Patrick and a special feature on the "Land of Lilliput", based on Jonathan Swift's most famous work, *Gulliver's Travels*. There is also a good local bookshop, and a café for tired bodies and aching feet. For those who wish to stay longer, the comparatively new Armagh City Hotel provides a good base for business and tourism.

Near the Trian at the heart of Armagh is the award-winning Market Place Theatre and Arts Centre which focuses on many of the area's cultural attractions. Armagh has a rich cultural history including the Armagh Rhymers. This is one of Northern Ireland's most colourful folk-theatre ensembles, carrying on a tradition dating back some 2,500 years. Armagh is also the home of J.B. Vallely, a noted Irish traditional musician and artist whose distinctive paintings are internationally acclaimed.

The former Archbishop's Palace, Robinson's palatial eighteenth-century residence, was once the home of the Church of Ireland Primates and is now the headquarters of the local Council. Within the large Palace Demesne there is an exhibition at the Stables Heritage Centre where guides dressed in Georgian livery relate the story of this historic place. Here too, is the extremely beautiful Primate's Chapel, which has been superbly restored and is regarded as one of the best examples of Georgian neo-classical architecture in Ireland.

At the entrance to the Demesne are the still-impressive remains of a thirteenth-century Franciscan Friary which was the longest in Ireland. Almost two miles west of Armagh just off the Caledon-Killylea Road is Navan Fort—the ancient site of Emain Macha—where archaeologists have found a rich heritage including traces of a huge Celtic temple.

"Navan" itself is a derivation of the ancient name of this settlement

Above: Exhibition on Ireland's patron saint at St. Patrick's Trian.

Above: The Land of Lilliput display at St. Patrick's Trian.

Left: Navan Fort, once the seat of power of Ulster's ancient kings.

which was mentioned by Ptolemy in a second-century map, and was a flourishing centre of activity at the time of Christ. According to scholars other Royal capitals in Ireland are Tara in Meath, Cruachain in Connacht and Dun Ailine in Leinster. A comparable site in Britain would be King Arthur's Camelot, base for the Knights of the Round Table, but the site for that has not yet firmly identified, whilst knowledge of the Irish Royal capitals has never been lost.

Emain Macha derives its title from a legendary war-goddess Macha—whose name is also perpetuated in Armagh—and has been described as the ancient capital of Ulster. It was the first named place in the history books and the seat of Ulster's ancient kings when her power was at its greatest. It was the pagan, spiritual and political centre of the Province. It was the geographical focus of its greatest works of literature and the first archaeological site in Northern Ireland to be nominated to UNESCO as a site of international importance.

Armagh also has a rich heritage from Celtic history. It is claimed that the main Irish sea-god Lir was mightily displeased at not being chosen as leader of the ancient De Danann, and he withdrew in a sulk to live on his own beneath a large mound known as Deadman's Hill, near Armagh city. This is marked by a stone cairn. Lir's isolation was relieved by his marriage to Aobh, the foster-daughter of the elected leader Bov. She bore him four children but died in child-birth. Lir was then offered her half-sister Aoife as a replacement. However she took umbrage at her step-children and with a druid wand turned them into swans—hence the tragic story of the Children of Lir, written in the fifteenth century but pre-dated by centuries of story-telling as a medieval legend known as the "Knight of the Swan."

Given the depth, richness and variety of the history in and around Armagh, it would be tempting to conclude this is the only worthwhile place to visit in the county. There is much else to enjoy in County Armagh, from its unspoilt countryside to the north bordering on Lough Neagh, to the vitality of its other main towns Portadown and Lurgan. Its numerous apple orchards give it the name of "the Orchard County," and the picturesque scenery in South Armagh, including the Model Village of Bessbrook, and the foothills of Camlough and Slieve Gullion are worth visiting.

To the north-east of Armagh at the heart of the apple orchards is the village of Loughgall, with its own Manor and Park, and a yew tree

Apple growing was introduced to County Armagh by seventeenth-century settlers from Worcestershire and their orchards were planted in the same pattern as the apple trees in the Vale of Evesham. The main bulk of the crop is Bramley cooking apples which the whole of Northern Ireland enjoys in delectable apple tarts and pies at Hallowe'en. In recent years mushroom growing has also taken off in the region.

Above: Apple-blossom time in Armagh.

walk which was planted in the early seventeenth century by the Cope family who settled there in 1610. Loughgall Country Park has an eighteen-hole golf course, a fishing lake, well-marked country walks and children's play area.

In the Diamond area there are two important historical landmarks. One is the ancestral home of Dan Winter which is also known as "the birthplace of the Orange Order." This is a listed building dating from the mid-eighteenth century and its comprehensive restoration in the year 2000 included the conservation of a large amount of the original fabric. The other historic building is an eighteenth-century thatched cottage on the site of the Battle of the Diamond between the Protestant Peep o' Day Boys and the Catholic Defenders in 1795. That same evening the victorious Protestants marched into Loughgall and formed the "Orange Society", later known as the Orange Order.

Right: Slieve Gullion countryside.

North of Loughall there are two elegant National Trust properties—one the homely Argory, a Victorian Mansion built in 1824, and housing a remarkable cabinet barrel organ and an early lighting system. The other is Ardress House, a seventeenth-century Plantation House with a nineteenth-century exterior, and what is regarded to be one of the finest classical drawing-rooms in Ireland. There is also an exhibition in the farmyard of historical machinery.

To the south and west of the Argory are the historic sites of Charlemont Fort and Benburb, which featured prominently in the Elizabethan battles of the late sixteenth and early seventeenth centuries. To the east are the modern towns of Portadown and Lurgan, which sadly were caught up in many of the battles of the recent Troubles.

Both towns were amalgamated in the mid-Sixties to form the then experimental "new town" of Craigavon, named after Northern Ireland's first Prime Minister James Craig, but it failed to establish itself in the way that the planners had hoped. Today Craigavon is a reality, but Portadown and Lurgan still retain their own distinct identities.

Portadown is a busy rural town, with friendly people, a wide shopping street and a great range of churches, including St. John the Baptist at Garvaghy Road and Drumcree Parish Church, the unfortunate focus of a long stand-off between Orangemen and local Nationalists which brought unwanted publicity to the area.

Portadown, however, has other claims to fame. It is the birthplace of Sir Robert Hart, who established the Post Office in China and who amassed a voluminous collection of diaries covering his fifty-four years overseas, which are now kept at the Queen's University of Belfast. Rather surprisingly he also introduced the Chinese to the joys of brass

Ardress House started life as a modest seventeenth-century farmhouse but when George Ensor married Sarah Clarke of Ardress in 1760 he decided to enlarge it adding an extra wing and a wall with dummy windows to the other side. The drawing-room was designed by Michael Stapleton, a celebrated stuccodore or plaster worker from Dublin, and features four beautiful plaques representing the seasons.

Above: Approach to Ardress House.

band music. Portadown was also the original home of the acclaimed rose-breeder Sam McGredy, who later settled in New Zealand.

Lurgan is another busy provincial town, which formerly played an important part in the textile industry. Its famous sons include the Irish man of art and letters George Russell (known as "AE") and James Logan, one of the founders of Pennsylvania. An equally famous "son" of Lurgan was Master McGrath, a greyhound owned by Lord Lurgan which won the Waterloo Cup three times between 1868 and 1871. He is commemorated not only by a stained-glass window in the local parish church, but also by the famous *Ballad of Master McGrath*, as well as a statue in the Craigavon Civic Centre. He is also represented in the local Coat of Arms.

Left: The Argory near Loughgall.

Brownlow House, Lord Lurgan's former residence, is a Tudor-style nineteenth-century mansion and is also the world headquarters of one of the Loyal Orders—the exquisitely named Imperial Grand Black Chapter of the British Commonwealth. The grounds are now a public park, with a golf course and a lake. The priceless Book of Armagh, the ninth-century manuscript which contains, among other works, the Life of St. Patrick, was "discovered" in the Brownlow library after having been pawned in 1680 by Florence MacMoyre for £5.

In a state of ill-repair, the book passed into the Brownlow's possession in 1707, where it remained until 1815 when the Reverend Francis Brownlow sent it on loan to the Royal Irish Academy in Dublin. In 1853 it was purchased by a Dr Reeves for £300, and sold without profit to the then Church of Ireland Primate Lord John George Beresford, who was also Chancellor of the University of Dublin. He presented it to the University library where it still remains. Given such a chequered history, the survival of the *Book of Armagh* is almost miraculous.

To the north of Lurgan lies Oxford Island and the Lough Neagh Discovery Centre, with a wildlife and nature reserve which highlights the area's large bird population and natural habitat. A colony of great crested grebe nest at Oxford Island and swans and herons also nest on the lough's islands. Lough Neagh is the largest fresh-water lake in the British Isles, and is a rich source for private and commercial fishing, especially for wild eels which swim up the Bann to reach the waters. Finn MacCool of Giant's Causeway fame is also said to be responsible for the creation of Lough Neagh. When he threw a clod of earth at his Scottish enemy the hole he left filled with water and became the lough. Finn was a bad shot and the clod of earth he threw missed its target and fell into the sea thus creating the Isle of Man.

Above: Brownlow House where the priceless *Book of Armagh* was "discovered."

Above: Oxford Island and the Lough Neagh Discovery Centre.

Right: Boats at Lough Neagh.

Moving south from Lurgan is Tandragee built on a steep hill beside the Cusher river. The town has been home to a castle for over three hundred years with the first castle being built by the O'Hanlon family. This was confiscated during the Plantation and in revenge the family later captured and destroyed it in 1641. The sixth Duke of Manchester built a new baronial-style castle around 1837 on the old site. The castle was turned into a crisp factory during the 1950s and given the new name of Tayto Castle! Visitors can see the famous Tayto crisps being made by arrangement.

To the west near Markethill is Gosford Forest Park, and in South Armagh is the "Model Village" of Bessbrook. This was established in 1845 around a local linen factory. John Grubb Richardson, a member of an English Quaker family, planned the village on the lines of a William Penn settlement, and it later inspired the Cadbury family to establish the garden township of Bournville, near Birmingham. The village was established without police, pawn-shops or public houses as it was hoped people wouldn't need or want them, and a rudimentary health care system was introduced—hence its description as a "Model Village."

Bessbrook was also well-known for its narrow gauge electric tramway, which was opened in October 1885. It had a maximum speed of 12 mph, and carried workers from Newry to the linen factory, as well as the general public. It was the second oldest of its kind in the British Isles, after the Portrush and Giant's Causeway tram. Sadly, however, with the decline in the linen business it closed after the Second World War.

Bessbrook, where this writer was born and brought up, retained its old-world charm until after the middle of the twentieth century when the decline of the linen-manufacturing business, and the resultant loss of employment, as well as the dubious advances of television and modern technology, and the Troubles, changed the face of the village for ever.

South of Bessbrook is the lovely scenery of South Armagh, with Camlough Lake and village, home of the former Evergreen football striker Graham McAleer. During the worst of the Troubles this countryside was virtually a no-go area for tourists, but today the whole area of Forkhill, Newtownhamilton and Crossmaglen is worth visiting, and particularly the Slieve Gullion Forest Park.

On the way back from Camlough and the Irish border region, the main road passes near the historic Derrymore House. Now in the care of the National Trust, this eighteenth-century thatched cottage was built by Isaac Corry (1755-1813). He was the MP for Newry in the Irish Parliament, and the last Chancellor of the Irish Exchequer. The Act of Union of 1800 was drafted in the drawing-room of this charming building.

The historic link between this area and Dublin is perpetuated even today, and not far from Derrymore House the 18-arch Craigmore Viaduct still carries the main railway line from Belfast to Dublin. The road leading away from South Armagh passes under the "Egyptian" Arch which was designed along the lines of a pylon of an Egyptian Temple. Further north is the "Frontier Town" of Newry and the gateway to the many attractions of County Down.

Above: Dean Swift's Well in Gosford Forest Park.

Left: Tandragee Castle now home to a crisp factory and renamed Tayto Castle!

Chapter 6

The Heart of Down

"Where the Mountains o' Mourne
Sweep down to the sea..."

Percy French

Left: The Mournes.

Above: The Mourne Wall.

These words from the celebrated nineteenth-century Irish song-writer Percy French who captured so winsomely the innocence of a bygone age, have made the Mourne Mountains and the County of Down world-famous. The song itself is a wistful lament of a young Irishman far from home and also a gentle satire on the London society in the late nineteenth century. It is said, however, that Percy French described the Mournes from the distant perspective of Skerries north of Dublin where, on a good day, they are visible on the skyline.

County Down stretches from the border city of Newry to the north of the Ards peninsula, and from Portavogie on the east coast to the almost-English rural beauty of Hillsborough. In between there are the many attractions of this varied county, ranging from the supposed burial-place of St. Patrick, in Downpatrick, to Strangford Lough and its many islands. On the way back to Belfast the main road passes the surburban elegance of parts of Holywood and Craigavad, which are sometimes called the "Gold Coast" of Northern Ireland.

Newry has very much the air of a "frontier" town and it is the traditional "Gap of the North". This was true not only for invading or retreating armies from the earliest of times, but also for tourists and shoppers in more recent years moving up from or down to Newry's twin Irish border town of Dundalk. Despite the lean years of the past Newry has an air of prosperity, and its recent elevation to the status of a city is a reflection of its growing self-esteem.

Newry Town Hall straddles the river border between Down and Armagh. The city has always been a "border" area and has many historic associations with past warlords, both English and Irish, and with nationalist politicians and writers. One of the best-known was the Irish Republican John Mitchel, a Protestant who was transported to Australia in the nineteenth century for treason, but who made one of the biggest political comebacks of the century. He escaped from Tasmania, went to America and then returned to Ireland to become MP for Tipperary. His statue in the town has the inscription "John Mitchel, 1815-1875. After twenty-seven years in exile for the sake of Ireland he returned with honour to die among his own people and he rests with his parents in the 1st Presbyterian Old Meeting House Green at Newry."

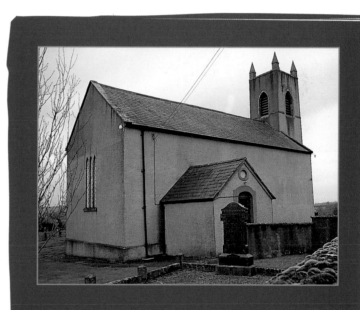

The Brontë Homeland Interpretive Centre near Rathfriland explains the connection between the celebrated Brontë sisters and Drumballyroney. Their father, Patrick Brunty was born between Banbridge and Rathfriland in 1777. The eldest of ten, he worked in the linen industry but continued to educate himself until finally in 1802 he enrolled at St John's College, Cambridge, changing his name to the now familiar Brontë. After graduating he preached and taught at Drumballyroney Church and School, later moving to England and eventually Haworth.

Above: Drumballyroney Church.

Left: Historic Newry Canal.

Newry has long been a significant commercial centre, particularly in the eighteenth century largely due to its elaborate inland canal system, which was one of the earliest in the British Isles.

Building of the canal finished in 1742 and the main cargoes being coal from Tyrone, local farming produce, granite from the Mournes, linen and even emigrants on the start of their long journey to America. Today the romantic names from the shipping past linger on, as in Sugar Island and Sugarhouse Quay, as well as Buttercrane Quay which gives its name to a large modern shopping-centre in the south of the city. One of the finest hotels in Northern Ireland is the nearby Canal Court, which has been developed imaginatively out of a former grain mill.

The coast road from Newry passes through beautiful scenery and past the prominent ruins of the sixteenth-century Narrow Water Castle, with the Carlingford Mountains to the south looking sometimes like a backdrop from the foothills of the Canadian Rockies. Carlingford, across the Lough in the Irish Republic, is readily accessible from Newry, and has recently become a much more up-market resort than in the past.

In former times when the border rules were more visibly enforced with British and Irish Customs posts situated on each side, there was a thriving smuggling trade between North and South—depending on which jurisdiction was currently favoured by the prevailing economy. There used to be a lively open-boat ferry across Carlingford Lough from Warrenpoint to Omeath, which was particularly busy on Sunday afternoons in spring and summer. Drinkers who could not find a pub open during the abstemious Northern Sabbath (legally at least) were willing to risk the often choppy sea crossing in order to slake their thirst and also try to smuggle back some cheap Irish bacon and sausages.

Warrenpoint is a tidy seaside town and a commercial port. Sadly, however, it has always had a stony beach, but the lack of sand is more than compensated for by the stunning views of the Mourne Mountains and Carlingford Lough. On the way to Rostrevor, a charming village in the foothills of the Mournes, there is a tall obelisk commemorating Major-General Robert Ross whose small contingent of troops captured the White House in Washington in 1814 and burned it to the ground. That once significant event is now an historical hiccup which does not disturb the excellent relationships between the USA and Northern Ireland today.

On the northern outskirts of Rostrevor is a path leading to the "Fiddler's Green," an attractive green clearing amid the trees which gives its name to an annual music festival in Rostrevor. The path leads on to the Cloughmore Stone—a glacial deposit weighing some forty tons and which sits in an area that provides panoramic views of the surrounding countryside. In the Rostrevor area a group of Benedictine monks from France have recently built a new monastery, thus reversing the general Western trend of decreased Christian worship and fewer churches.

Above: Narrow Water Castle on Carlingford Lough.
Right: Rocks carved by erosion on Slieve Commedagh.

The twisting but negotiable main road winds erratically along the coast, and a little inland, to reach the fishing ports of Kilkeel and Annalong where the Mourne Mountains provide a picturesque backdrop to this sea faring and rural charm.

Despite the beautiful scenery, the job of commercial fisherman remains a difficult and dangerous occupation, and the industry is facing hard times because of EC fishing restrictions and regulations.

The restored Annalong Corn Mill is the last of its kind in the Mournes. It operated from about 1830 until 1960, and was powered by a water wheel—and latterly by a 1920's engine. The restoration work began in 1983, with the support of the local Newry and Mourne District Council. It is now open to the public, and nearby there is a visitors centre and parking facilities.

The so-called "Kingdom of Mourne", with its poetic mountain names like Slievenagore, Slievenalogh, Slieve Loughshannagh, Slieve Bearnagh, Slievecoragh, Slievelamagan, Slieve Binnian and Wee Binnian, and the larger Slieve Martin, Slieve Muck and Slieve Donard, is almost a place apart. It is a kingdom of fields enclosed by intricate dry-stone walls, of gorse and sturdy grazing animals, a place of legend and folk-lore, with stunning views of the many peaks of the Mournes, and above all with canny and friendly people.

It is said that parts of Hyde Park Corner in London and the approach to Buckingham Palace are composed of Mourne granite, and Mourne fishermen and sailors have graced the oceans all around the world. There were hard times in the Mournes, and it was the sea and the land which contributed so much to the staple diet of fish and chips at a time when food was not as varied or as plentiful as it is today.

The Mourne countryside is accessible by motor transport from a number of different areas, and a good map is useful for touring. Vehicles have access to the southern end of the Silent Valley Reservoir, which supplies the city of Belfast with millions of gallons of water every day, and there is an air of tranquility about this place, as well as beautiful scenery.

Right: The Silent Valley Reservoir in the heart of the Mournes.

On the far side of Slieve Muck, through the mountains by way of the B27 from Kilkeel to Hilltown, is the Spelga Dam, which also has impressive views over the Mourne foothills. This entire area provides many challenges for walkers of varying stamina and skill, and these range from pleasant strolls to the much tougher challenges of the craggier peaks including Slieve Donard, the highest at nearly 2,800 feet. As with all forms of climbing, common sense and care are necessary, with a wary eye kept on the approaching weather. There are lists of well-documented trails, which should be available in local shops and tourist offices.

The town of Newcastle, with the excellent recreation area of Tollymore Forest Park near the attractive village of Bryansford, provides an ideal base for touring the Mourne country, either in a vehicle or for shorter treks on foot. Those who want challenging exercise of a different kind might consider a round of golf at Royal County Down which is rightly regarded by experts as one of the best golf courses in the world. Those who have the money and the skill to take on such a challenge might even encounter exotic visitors such as the film stars Michael Douglas and Catherine Zeta Jones, and champion golfers like Jack Nicklaus, who have all played there at various times.

Around the corner from the golf course is the Slieve Donard Hotel, with magnificent views of the long Newcastle beach and the mountain whose name it bears. Each summer the Donegal singing-star and entertainer Daniel O' Donnell plays to full houses in the Hotel, and also hones his skill on the golf course. Also on summer Sundays the Newcastle main street is full of motorbikes and bikers, while the music of groups like Baillie's Mills Accordion Band wafts across the promenade.

Sadly, Newcastle still lacks an adequate memorial to Percy French, the man who put the Mountains of Mourne so firmly on the world map. However, there is an inscribed stone on the promenade wall which commemorates the 1910 flight along the beach by the inventor Harry Ferguson in his home-made monoplane—for which he collected

The Mourne Wall stretching high into the mountains was built over eighteen years, from 1904 to 1922, to enclose the 9,000 acres of mountainside which drain into the Silent Valley and Ben Crom reservoirs. Rising and falling over fifteen mountains including Slieve Donard and Slieve Binnian the wall was built by local men, some of whom even camped on site under sail-cloth and went home mid-week for supplies. It is said that when Friday came the men did not stop running until they reached Annalong and home.

Above: The Mourne Wall.

Above: Mountain sheep graze the banks of Shanky's River.

Below: A new day over the Silent Valley.

Above: Red sky over Altataggart Mountain.

Below: The summit cairn of Lamagan.

the princely sum of £100.

North-east of Newcastle is the village of Dundrum, with the Buck's Head Restaurant, and along the coast is the extensive Murlough Nature Reserve. To the north-west of Newcastle on the A50 road is Castlewellan, in its own right an interesting place with noteworthy squares, churches and market-houses.

However the main attraction is the comprehensive Forest Park and National Arboretum which was established in the mid-eighteenth century and developed by the local Annesley landlords from the late nineteenth century. This is one of the most beautiful of its kind in these islands, with a three-mile route around a picturesque lake, ample parking and other facilities. The Arboretum has an absolutely outstanding collection of trees, plants and flowers of all kinds. It is particularly beautiful in spring when the rhododendrons are in bloom and also when the varied autumn colours are on display.

Above: Down Cathedral in Downpatrick.

Right: Shimna River in Tollymore Forest Park.

Downpatrick has an impressive Church of Ireland Cathedral, dating in various versions from the thirteenth century. Like Armagh Cathedral and many others it suffered damage from repeated incursions in local wars, but it is perhaps unique in that it was damaged by an earthquake in 1245—a particularly rare event in Ireland.

The Cathedral has an impressive organ case, and an organ was given to the church by King George III in the early nineteenth century. It is said that John Wesley, the eighteenth-century evangelist and Church of England clergyman who founded Methodism was banned from preaching in Anglican pulpits, but he solved this problem easily in Downpatrick by preaching just outside the Cathedral.

Near the building there is a tenth-century High Cross, and nearby is reputedly the burial-place of St. Patrick, the Patron saint of Ireland, and also two other Irish saints, Columba and Brigid—though the latter are much less associated with the place than is Patrick. Most scholars agree that he landed on the County Down coast near Saul where he began his mission to Ireland in the fifth century, and where an attractive little Anglican church with a round tower stands today.

There is also a huge stone memorial statue of St. Patrick which dominates the countryside near Saul. However, historians are not quite so clear that he was actually buried in nearby Downpatrick, despite the large heart-shaped gravestone with a cross and the lettering 'Patric' which is embedded in the ground near the Cathedral. According to a local tradition, people used to scoop up handfuls of earth from Patrick's supposed burial place, with the result that the site was marked by a dip in the ground. A large granite stone placed there in 1902 by the instigation of Francis Joseph Bigger and his friends from the Belfast Naturalists' Field Club ended such practices, and it remains a memorial to this remarkable Christian, whether he was actually buried there or not.

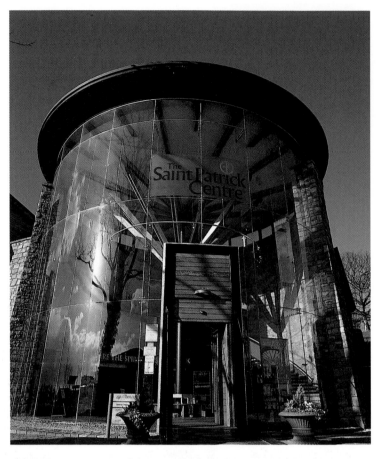

Above: The Saint Patrick Centre tells the story of Patrick's life and work.

Above: One of several suggested locations for St. Patrick's Grave.

There are hundreds of legends about Patrick, including the claim that was given yet another airing, by Bigger himself, in the Belfast Telegraph on the eve of St. Patrick's Day in 1923.

According to this legend, St. Patrick's body was placed on a raised bier yoked to four white oxen. It was said that they wound their way from the old Abbey of Saul, and the place where they eventually decided to stop was chosen as his burial place, around which a town developed. Other legends claim that Patrick lived until he was 120, and that on his death there was darkness over the earth for several days.

However, those who want more reliable information on Ireland's Patron Saint should visit the excellent St. Patrick's Centre in Downpatrick. This recently-opened historical and visitor complex has an excellent audio-visual display and exhibition which sets his life and mission in context, amid the stunning scenery of the region.

There are a number of attractive Georgian buildings near the Cathedral, and on hilly English Street is Denvir's Hotel, established in 1642, and still dispensing good cheer and hospitality. The Down County Museum was formerly an eighteenth-century gaol where the United Irishman Thomas Russell was hanged 1803 for alleged conspiracy against the English. A memorial stone to Russell was placed in the parish church graveyard by Mary Anne McCracken, the sister of another leading Republican figure Henry Joy McCracken who was captured for his part in the 1798 Rebellion and hanged at Cornmarket in Belfast on 17 July.

The County Museum has an authentically restored Governor's house, and still has the cells which detained convicts prior to their deportation. Ironically many Irish "convicts" flourished in their new territory–and many spectacularly so in Australia–but irrespective of their crimes whether real or alleged, it is sad to reflect today on the hardship suffered by those forced to leave, and the loss to their families who in most cases would never see them again.

Moving along the track we come to a much more innocent

dimension of Downpatrick's history, the Railway Museum, near the site of the original station. Steam enthusiasts have restored a two-mile section of the old Belfast and County Down Railway, and it is worth visiting to see the various locomotives and carriages, and the workshop where the restoration of older stock continues.

A prominent feature is the rebuilt railway station itself, which has been reconstructed from materials taken from a contemporary building. An aspiring train-driver (an occupation that was the dream of generations of small boys before the age of space travel) can enrol here on a six-hour training course. After passing the final test, the new train-driver can take his or her place proudly on the locomotive's footplate, and friends can travel free in the carriages!

Transport of a different kind of features prominently at the former RAF airfield at Bishopscourt, some six miles south of Downpatrick, where motor-cycle races are held along the old perimeter tracks and runway. Another former RAF airfield at Kirkistown, across Strangford Lough on the Ards peninsula, is also a popular venue for motorcycle racing, and hosts national and international competitions.

In the Lecale region east of Bishopscourt, the road leads to Struell Wells with its reputation for miraculous healing from ancient times, and further along, the B1 road reaches the fishing port of Ardglass, with its relatively new marina. This is a village with a whiff of history, with the fifteenth-century Jordan's Castle prominent against the skyline. Much later, in the early twentieth century, it was purchased and restored, and later filled with antiques by the same publicly-spirited Francis Joseph Bigger who, only a few years earlier, had been one of the driving forces in placing a stone over St. Patrick's supposed burial-spot. Mr Bigger donated the Castle to the Government for posterity, and the tower-house is still open to the public in summer. South-west of Ardglass is St. John's Point with panoramic views of the Mourne Mountains and Dundrum Bay.

Above: One of the bath-houses at Struell Wells.

Next Page: Sunset over Strangford Lough.

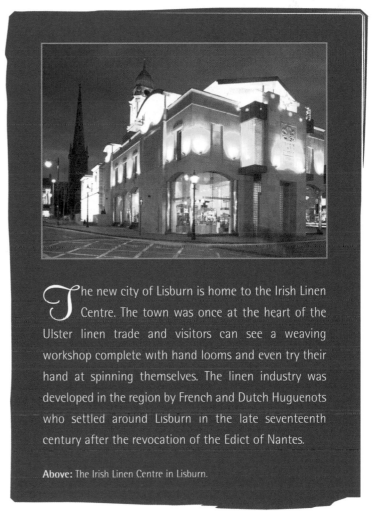

The new city of Lisburn is home to the Irish Linen Centre. The town was once at the heart of the Ulster linen trade and visitors can see a weaving workshop complete with hand looms and even try their hand at spinning themselves. The linen industry was developed in the region by French and Dutch Huguenots who settled around Lisburn in the late seventeenth century after the revocation of the Edict of Nantes.

Above: The Irish Linen Centre in Lisburn.

On the circular drive back to Downpatrick by way of Chapeltown and the village of Ballyhornan, beside Gun's Island and also near a nature reserve at Killard Point, the road reaches the fifteenth-century Kilclief Castle, one of the oldest tower-houses in Ireland. The attractive village of Strangford, at the southeastern entrance to the Lough of the same name, provides a wonderful panorama around the Lough and across to Portaferry, to which it is linked by a regular vehicle and passenger ferry.

This is an all-too-short crossing with spectacular views, but the strong currents swirling in and out of the Lough demand skill and experience from the crew of the ferry. Perhaps even more skill, and endurance, was required in earlier times when livestock were ferried across the often-choppy waters in open craft. Such boatmanship was remarkable, given that some 400 million tons of tidal water move through the narrows at the end of the inlet, twice a day. No wonder the Vikings called it, "the violent ford."

On the way back from Strangford to Downpatrick, the road passes Castle Ward, which is under the care of the National Trust. It was named after its first owners, the Ward family and was built in the early eighteenth century.

Above: Gothic-style architecture at Castle Ward favoured by Lady Bangor.
Right: The Palladian front of Castle Ward chosen by her husband, Lord Bangor.

It is also a monument to the remarkable marital and architectural compromise between the strong-minded Lord and Lady Bangor. He chose classic Palladian for the front, while she favoured a Gothic style elsewhere. Her boudoir, with its vaulted ceiling based on Henry VIII's Chapel at Westminster Abbey, can best be described as "cluttered", or in the Ulster idiom "a bit through-other."

Apart from the always fascinating but in parts claustrophobic building, Castle Ward has splendid gardens, a large park with excellent walks, and an intriguing and still functional corn mill.

There is also a small theatre in one of the out-buildings, where the Castle Ward Opera regularly stages productions of good quality. Back in Downpatrick, the visitor can turn inland to discover the attractions of the county west of Strangford Lough, which will be described along with the rest of the Ards peninsula later on in this chapter. Crossgar was the home town of the twentieth-century inventor Sir James Martin, who established the Martin-Baker Aircraft Company and developed a series of aircraft which equaled, if not bettered, the famous World War II Spitfire and Hurricane. Among his many inventions, the most famous was the Martin-Baker ejector seat, which was adapted by airforces around the world, and which has saved the lives of many thousands of pilots and other aircrew.

The B2 road leads to Ballynahinch, which has much history associated with the 1798 Rebellion, like Saintfield nearby. On the road north to Belfast, about a mile from Saintfield, is the magnificent estate of Rowallane, the headquarters of the National Trust in Northern Ireland. It is one of the significant gardens of the British Isles, and the previous owner, Hugh Armitage Moore, spent more than half-a-century creating a spectacular landscape out of the 50 acres around the mansion. There are fascinating floral, plant and tree displays according to the season, and in springtime Rowallane is particularly full of colour when the rhododendrons and azaleas are in full bloom. The walled garden is also attractive, with its seasonal roses, poppies, lilies and autumn plants.

Rowallane has a number of stimulating walks around the grounds, and there is a restaurant for those who need refreshments after their rambles. A proposed innovation is the inclusion of a Pierrot Bandstand

for musical performances, to make up for the loss of the much-prized structure which used to grace Newcastle's promenade many years ago. It even had real "pierrots" singing that hardy annual *There's no business like show-business*, despite the seasonal chill of an Ulster summer.

In fact the sound of music is never far away in Northern Ireland, and the tradition of self-entertainment continues to thrive, as it did in earlier generations.

Whether the style is Irish traditional music, folk and country, or old-tyme, enthusiastic groups play in all sorts of places, ranging from church halls to pubs and even in each other's homes. The lively tones of a fiddle, accordion, flute, whistle and other instruments lift the spirit, and the shared joy of music and a common harmony and humanity crosses all boundaries, religious and otherwise.

This is nowhere more apparent than in Kilmood, between Killinchy and Ballygowan, where the Music Club holds weekly sessions in a church hall. These attract large audiences in a relaxed atmosphere where instrumentalists and story-tellers are always welcome. Early attendance is recommended for those who want a good seat.

From there it is a comparatively short journey to Comber, a still-attractive town within commuting distance of Belfast but which is not yet spoilt by over-development. It has a Georgian square, dominated by a large monument to Sir Robert Rollo Gillespie, an eighteenth-century Major General and a Knight Commander of "the Most Honourable Military Order of the Bath." The exploits of this Comber-born adventurer could form the basis of a stirring novel or a television epic.

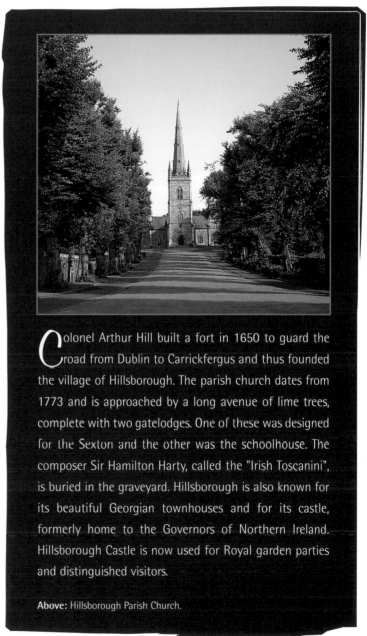

Colonel Arthur Hill built a fort in 1650 to guard the road from Dublin to Carrickfergus and thus founded the village of Hillsborough. The parish church dates from 1773 and is approached by a long avenue of lime trees, complete with two gatelodges. One of these was designed for the Sexton and the other was the schoolhouse. The composer Sir Hamilton Harty, called the "Irish Toscanini", is buried in the graveyard. Hillsborough is also known for its beautiful Georgian townhouses and for its castle, formerly home to the Governors of Northern Ireland. Hillsborough Castle is now used for Royal garden parties and distinguished visitors.

Above: Hillsborough Parish Church.

Above: The music group in action at Kilmood.
Left: The gates leading into Hillsborough Fort.

He was a cavalryman who was involved in duels, shipwrecks, amorous adventures and bloody military engagements before being shot through the head at Kalunca in the Himalayas. His final words, faithfully recorded on the plinth of his statue, were "One more shot for the honour of Down."

Comber is also associated with another figure who made the headlines in his day. It was the home of Thomas Andrews, the former managing director of the Harland and Wolff shipyard and the chief designer of the *Titanic*. He sailed with the ship on its maiden voyage and was one of the hundreds drowned in the tragedy. The family residence "Ardara" was recently converted to apartments.

In its heyday Comber was an industrial centre noted for linen and whiskey, and it even had two distilleries. One was known as "Old Comber", which was said to rival "Old Bushmills" distilled in County Antrim, and Comber whiskey featured long in the experience of those with a discerning taste for spirits of the liquid kind.

The road from Comber leads across the hills, amid beautiful scenery to Crawfordsburn Country Park where there is an attractive walk, a viaduct, a waterfall and a sandy beach. Nearby is the Old Inn at Crawfordsburn, dating from 1614 and still with old-world charm, and

an occasional sighting of the Ulster singer and song-writer Van Morrison.

Near Holywood, with its annual jazz festival and its trendy shops and restaurants, and the only Maypole in Ireland, is the outstanding Ulster Folk and Transport Museum. Here the visitor might usefully spend a whole day or more exploring the story of the development of the Province in terms of its architecture, its social and family life and its transport.

The Folk Museum has been evolving and developing since the late Fifties and is set in the graceful Cultra Manor estate.

Many of the historic buildings on display have been removed and transported from their earlier sites, often literally brick by brick. They include rural farmhouses and buildings, a blacksmith's forge, churches, whole terraces from urban areas, and much much more. The authenticity of the Ulster Folk Museum was underlined by this writer's grandfather Thomas McCreary who, on being taken to see a nineteenth-century rural cottage, said "There's nothing new here. Sure I lived in a cottage like that!"

Across the main Belfast-Bangor road is the Transport Museum, which itself is a treasure of artefacts from earlier days. It includes a Model T Ford and a De Lorean gull-wing DMC 12 car, which had a dramatic and exotic history, like the man who invented it.

There are reminders of Northern Ireland's outstanding engineering and aeronautical successes, including the Sunderland flying-boat and the Shorts Skyvan, and also the innovative but ill-fated *Titanic* which, in one sense, has remained essentially afloat in the imagination of all who still marvel at such a stunning engineering achievement for the early twentieth century. Today the vessels plying in and out of Belfast, including the most modern ferries, travel the same waters down which the *Titanic* proudly sailed so long ago. As with so much else in the Ulster story, the past and the present live cheek by jowl. Who knows what outstanding developments and inventions will be on display a hundred years from now...

Above: Part of the Irish Railway Collection at the Ulster Transport Museum.

Right: A demonstration of how life used to be at the Ulster Folk Museum.

THE ARDS PENINSULA AND STRANGFORD

Bangor, at the northern end of the Ards peninsula, is an attractive seaside resort and a commuter town some 12 miles from Belfast. It has pleasant promenade walks, good beaches and the largest marina in Ireland.

Historically it is closely associated with the Irish Saints like Columbanus and Gall who helped to keep alive the flame of Christianity in the Europe of the Dark Ages.

According to tradition the Abbot of Bangor defended the Celtic Church so strongly at the Council of Whitby in 664 AD that Saint Augustine's spokesman remarked that Bangor has "opposed all the rest of the universe." Clearly this was the earliest-recorded version of a recent political slogan "Ulster says No." But, if Bangor carried a Christian flame of hope to Europe so long ago, it was perhaps fitting that Europe brought the Olympic "Flame of Hope" to Bangor in 2003 for the World Special Olympics in Ireland.

Nothing remains of the Abbey which St. Comgall founded in 558 AD, or of two twelfth-century monasteries, except a small part of a wall near the fifteenth-century parish church and possibly a sundial at the Castle. The Abbey was plundered by Vikings in the ninth century and the story of the region is told in the North Down Heritage Centre in the Castle Park. The Bangor Hand Bell, made of solid Bronze and found in the old Abbey graveyard, is also on display there.

East of Bangor the road leads along the attractive coastline to Groomsport and Donaghadee, where pictures of the local lighthouse and harbour have graced countless calendars. Offshore are the Copeland Islands, with their own famous lighthouse and bird sanctuary. The main road leads due south along the coast through Millisle, near the eye-catching Ballycopeland Windmill. At Ballywalter is the local estate of Lord Dunleath, and a charming and tiny eighteenth-century Church of St. Andrew at Balligan, which is well-known for the quality of its recitals.

South of Ballyhalbert is the fishing village of Portavogie, noted for its quayside fish auctions. Portaferry at the southern tip of Strangford Lough has a graceful seafront, as well as the excellent Exploris Aquarium.

The road from Portaferry leads north along the east shore of Strangford Lough and through the neat village of Greyabbey, the site of a twelfth-century Cistercian church founded by the wife of

Above: Ballycopeland Windmill on the coast near Millisle.
Left: Yachts and sailing-boats in Bangor Marina.
Next Page: The formal gardens at Mount Stewart.

John De Courcy, the Norman war-lord who ruled Ulster. The gravestones include those of '"Geo Matthews, born Feb. 27,1818, and perished in the wreck of the steamship Tweed...in the Gulf of Mexico, February 12, 1847", and also of a "Captain Hugh Bernard Montgomery wounded at Waterloo, June 18, 1815."

At Mount Stewart, on the shores of Strangford Lough, there are reminders of the Napoleonic period and much else, in one of the great National Trust stately homes and gardens of the British Isles.

Mount Stewart is an eighteenth-century building with nineteenth-century additions, and was the boyhood home of Lord Castlereagh, the British Foreign Secretary during the Napoleonic Wars. The house has many fascinating furnishings and historic objects, including the twenty-two chairs used at the Congress of Vienna from 1815-16, The Hambeltonian painted in 1799 by George Stubbs, the hooves of the race-horse Fightin' Charlie which won the Gold Cop with jockey Lester Piggott, and a porcelain figure of a German soldier presented by one of Hitler's associates during a visit just before the Second World War.

The gardens at Mount Stewart are truly magnificent, and they include a Shamrock Garden, with a yew tree enclosing an Irish harp, the beautifully-landscaped Sunken Garden which is a myriad of colours in Spring and Summer, and a Spanish Garden with neat rows of cypress trees. There is also the Dodo Terrace with its stone ark and dodos representing members of the Ark Club. This was established by the exotic Lady Londonderry who transformed the gardens in the early twentieth century and laid the foundations for their continuing beauty.

Mount Stewart also has an excellent lake walk, a good restaurant, and in spring and summer a jazz band on specified weekends. There is also a late eighteenth-century "Temple of the Winds" designed by "Athenian Stuart", which has a spiral staircase and affords commanding views over Strangford Lough. At nearby Carrowdore the Ulster poet Louis MacNeice is buried in the local graveyard.

The main road winds past the north-east of Strangford Lough, with its excellent bird sanctuary and leads to the market town of Newtownards, which lies beyond a small airfield where the Ulster Air Show takes place each June. Newtownards is also the home of the world-famous Dickson's roses, and the commercial radio station Downtown is based at Kiltonga estate.

Near Newtownards is Scrabo Tower, one of the Province's best-known landmarks. It was built in the mid-nineteenth century by grateful tenants in memory of the third Marquis of Londonderry who helped to relieve the effects of the famine, and it provides sweeping views over Strangford Lough and most of North Down. Beside the Tower is Scrabo Golf Club where the hilly course requires not only skill but stamina. One of the rewards (few enough for most amateur golfers) is the stunning view.

Above: The still-impressive ruins of Grey Abbey.

Left: Scrabo Tower overlooks Strangford Lough.

Above: Killyleagh Castle.

egananny Dolmen with its distinctive tripod shape is around 4,000 years old, dating to the Neolithic age. The ancient tomb is near Slieve Croob and is worth seeking out for its view of the Mournes.

Above: Neolithic Legananny Dolmen.

At nearby Clandeboye, the historic seat of the Dufferin and Ava family, is Helen's Tower. This was built in the mid-nineteenth century in honour of Helen, Lady Dufferin, and a replica tower stands near at Thiepval in France, where the 36th (Ulster) Division suffered such carnage at the Battle of the Somme in 1916. Prior to the war the Ulstermen had trained at Clandeboye, near Helen's Tower. The Somme Heritage Centre sets these tragic events, and the courage of all those involved, in sombre historical perspective, and it provides an important contribution to an integral part of the Ulster story.

On the west of Strangford Lough is Castle Espie, with its waterfowl gardens and woodland walks, and on Mahee Island is Nendrum, founded by St. Mochaoi in the fifth century. On the west of the island is Captain Browne's Castle, dating from the fifteenth century. At Sketrick Island there is a restaurant with character, named Daft Eddie's after a local smuggler of former days.

At Killyleagh the local Castle dates from the seventeenth century, with a silhouette that is more the Loire Valley than rural Ulster. Near the Castle there is a memorial to Sir Hans Sloane "born at Killyleagh 1660, President of the Royal College of Physicians, President of the Royal Society, Physician, Botanist, and Bibliophile, whose extensive collections formed the nucleus of the British Museum."

This under-stated curriculum vitae underlines so much of the charm and surprise of any journey around Northern Ireland—at almost every corner there is a story, a historic stone or plaque, a brilliant invention or yet another stunning view. This Province and its people, and their visitors, have much indeed to celebrate.